SMART SKILLS BUILDER

ICT

STUDENT'S BOOK

2nd Edition

SMART LEARNING

SMART SKILLS BUILDER

I C T

YR8 Student's Book
2nd Edition

Smart Learning Limited
P.O. Box 321
Cambridge, CB1 2XU
Tel: 01223 477550
Fax: 01223 477551
Website: www.smart-learning.co.uk

Acknowledgements

Authors: Original materials by Melanie Burtoft, Patricia Garvey, Emma Henderson, Kathryn Kelly, Tricia Lockhart
Additional materials by Chris Pim and Mike Adams
Series consultants: Margaret Derrington and Tricia Lockhart
Design by Billin Design Solutions and Matthew Lilly

Software and website screenshots

Microsoft product screenshots reprinted with permission from Microsoft Corporation; Adobe® Dreamweaver® product screenshots reprinted with permission from Adobe Systems Incorporated (pages 25–32); Weather data table © Crown copyright 2007, data supplied by the Met Office (page 5); Environment Agency website screenshot reproduced by permission of the Environment Agency (page 15); Natural History Museum website screenshots © The Natural History Museum, London reproduced with permission (page 22); DEFRA website screenshot reproduced under the terms of the Click-Use Licence (page 22); Snow Patrol website screenshot © Snow Patrol, reproduced with permission (page 23); Google™ and Google™ Earth screenshots, reproduced by permission of Google UK (pages 7, 21, 39, 40, 41, 42); PETA leaflet, reproduced by permission of PETA (page 40); Scratch screenshots reproduced by permission of the Lifelong Kindergarten Group at the MIT Media Lab (website: http://scratch.mit.edu) (pages 70–86); Amazon screenshot © www.amazon.co.uk, reproduced by permission (page 92); FlashMeeting screenshots © copyright KMi, The Open University UK working with E2BN – The East of England Broadband Network (pages 93–94); Audacity® software is copyright © 1999–2008 Audacity Team, it is free software distributed under the terms of the GNU General Public License, the name Audacity® is a registered trademark of Dominic Mazzoni (website: http://audacity.sourceforge.net) (pages 95–96).

Illustrations

Tim Davies for pages 1–20; Tony Forbes for pages 21–36; Rory Walker for pages 37–52; James Hofton for The Factoids website design, pages 29, 32, 36; Jo Taylor for pages 53–68; Matthew Lilly for cover (left) and pages 69–86; John Haslam for pages 87–106.

Photographs

Cover photographs © Getty Images; background photographs © iStockphoto
Jason Billin and Matt Lilly for page 92; Getty Images for pages 2, 3 (bottom right), 6, 45, 46, 48, 79
iStockphoto for pages 1, 3 (top right), 28, 29, 32, 33, 35, 36, 40 (bottom right), 42, 47, 51, 52, 53, 54, 56, 73, 80, 88, 89, 90, 95, 105; Tricia Lockhart for page 3 (centre right).

British Library Cataloguing-in-Publication Data
A CIP record for this book is available from the British Library

ISBN 978-1-84276-118-2

Printed in the UK by The Burlington Press Limited, Station Road, Foxton, Cambridge CB22 6SW

Please note: This book contains links to websites that are not maintained by Smart Learning. Although we make every effort to ensure these links are accurate, up-to-date and appropriate, Smart Learning cannot take responsibility for the content of any external websites.

Introduction

Welcome to the **Year 8 Smart Skills Builder for ICT Student's Book**. This book is designed to help you develop many of the key skills you need to excel in your ICT lessons and beyond! As you work through the book, you will be given a range of exciting scenarios and fun themes to practise your skills around, from designing a website for a band, to designing a computer game.

Units

The book contains six themed units, each of which is built around a series of tutorials, which introduce you to software, skills, concepts and key terms. You will also find an assessment activity and model answers at the end of each unit.

When you start each unit, you should set up a folder in your area to store all your work for that unit. Each time you create a new document, you should save it in this folder, so you can find it again easily.

Tutorials

Each tutorial contains a series of numbered steps to guide you easily through a range of practical ICT skills, such as downloading data from the internet, building a website, editing digital video clips and recording a podcast.

CD Resources

You will find references to CD Resources in many of the tutorials. These provide additional activities, templates and resources for you to complete as you work through the unit. Your teacher will be able to tell you where you can find these.

Unit assessments

At the end of all the units there is a unit assessment activity. This is an assessed piece of work, based on the skills you will have learned during the unit. You should complete this activity on your own so that your teacher can see what skills you have learned, and what level you are working at.

Model Answers

Model answers at Levels 5 and 6 are provided at the end of each unit. These allow you to see how you can improve your work and raise your level.

**We hope that you enjoy working through the activities
provided in this Smart Skills Builder for ICT!**

Teachers: This Smart Skills Builder for ICT Student's Book is designed to be used in conjunction with the Smart Skills Builder for ICT Teacher's Book and CD-ROM.

Contents

Unit introduction

The Go Green Travel Company is a travel company promoting greener holidays to teenagers and young adults.

Tourism is a major contributor to global warming and environmental damage. Planes produce CO_2 emissions, one of the major 'greenhouse gases' that cause global warming. Animals' habitats are destroyed to make way for luxury hotels for foreign tourists. Despite all of this, it seems that more and more people go on foreign holidays every year.

Go Green's owners want to make young people aware of these issues, and provide them with an alternative kind of holiday. And guess what – they want you to help them!

Unit learning objectives

We are learning to:

- Research different types of public information systems
- Understand what sensors are and how they are used
- Collect data automatically in a variety of ways
- Present and update information
- Use statistical functions of a spreadsheet to analyse data
- Learn how analysis has led to identification of patterns such as global warming
- Subscribe to, and set up, an RSS feed
- Use Google™ Earth, and export data in a variety of forms

Unit preparation

1. You will need to set up a folder in your area and name it **Unit 8.1 – Environmental Tourists**.

2. You will need to know the basic functions of a spreadsheet.

Start thinking about ...

Information presentation

Information must be displayed in a way that is appropriate for the people who will be using it.

What would be important to think about if you were designing a system for displaying traffic information on a motorway?

If you were designing a system for presenting messages to people in an international airport, what would be one thing you would need to consider? What would be a good way of displaying information for an international audience?

Step 1.1

Find the information you need

What sort of information do tourists usually want when they are planning a holiday? Make a list with a partner.

Then decide which information from your list you could find in the places shown on the right.

Which information needs to be completely up-to-date? What would be the best sources to get up-to-date information?

Step 1.2

Up-to-date information

Nowadays we are used to being able to access all the up-to-date information we need: from flight times to what the local weather is in Barbados this morning.

If these systems were not updated regularly, the information in them would be useless, and could cause chaos for travellers!

Systems that provide this sort of regularly updated information are called **public information systems**.

Step 1.3

Public information systems

A public information system works in three steps. Think of a weather station system:

1. First it must **obtain** the raw data (such as rainfall, atmospheric pressure).
2. Next it must **process** the information, changing it into something more understandable by people.
3. Finally, it must **present** the processed data so it is understandable and appropriate for its audience.

These three steps can be simplified to:

Input ⟶ Process ⟶ Output

Step 1.4

GIGO – garbage in, garbage out!

If the data that is **input** into the system is wrong, the information that is **output** will probably also be wrong.

GIGO: garbage in – garbage out

It is very important that the data inputted into a public information system is correct in order to give the public the correct information.

Environmental Tourists

UNIT

Tutorial 2 Sensors and datalogging

Environmental friendliness begins at home! The owners of The Go Green Travel Company want to make sure that their shop is not wasting too much energy. They want you to log (record) information about temperature and light levels, and advise them on how they might reduce these to be more environmentally friendly.

By the end of this tutorial you will be able to:

- Understand the difference between analogue and digital sensors
- Carry out basic analysis of logged data and create a chart

Step 2.1

What is a sensor?

A sensor is a piece of equipment that senses or monitors something. A common example is a thermometer, which is a temperature sensor. Others include movement sensors, pressure sensors, humidity sensors and smoke detectors. There are two different types of sensor – **analogue** sensors and **digital** sensors.

Step 2.2

Analogue sensors

Analogue sensors can measure over a **continuous** range and their readings may form a curve. A mercury thermometer is an analogue sensor that senses changes in temperature through the expansion of mercury.

If an analogue sensor is used as a computer input, a device must be used to convert the analogue signal to a digital format. This device is known as an 'analogue to digital converter'.

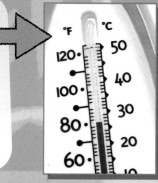

Step 2.3

Digital sensors

Digital sensors jump between values, though if the steps are small, they may not be detected by the human eye.

Modern desk weather systems can detect values from wireless sensors and can store data over a period of time.

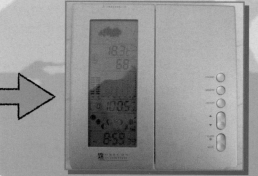

Step 2.4

Datalogging

When sensors are attached to a computer that records readings at intervals over time, this is known as **datalogging**.

Sometimes readings are sent to another remote computer by wireless or satellite. At the North and South Poles, the equipment might be inaccessible for months, so the data may be stored at the site until it can be retrieved some time later.

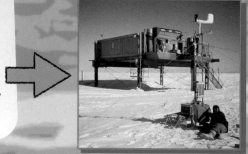

Tutorial 2   Sensors and datalogging

Step 2.5

Input data

If your school has datalogging equipment, your teacher can set this up and use it to log temperature and light levels in your classroom. If you don't have datalogging equipment, use **CD Resource 2d**, which shows sample light and temperature data logged in the Go Green shop.

The data is organised into columns. The first column shows the time at which the data was logged. The next columns show the data recorded – in this example, temperature and light levels.

Step 2.6

Analyse data to find useful information

When a lot of data is logged over time, it can be difficult to spot trends or patterns. There are ways in which you can extract useful information from a large dataset.

Scroll down the sheet to the last recorded entry. Then type labels in the first column as shown in the screenshot on the right.

Step 2.7

Calculate maximum, minimum and average values

To calculate the highest, lowest and average values in a spreadsheet, you need to type in formulae as follows:

Average value   =AVERAGE(first cell:last cell)

Minimum value   =MIN(first cell:last cell)

Maximum value   =MAX(first cell:last cell)

Range is the difference between the minimum and maximum values. Can you write a formula to work this out?

Step 2.8

Present data as a chart

When a lot of data is being recorded, a chart or graph can be a useful way of showing a trend (the way in which something changes over time). Which chart type is best for showing a trend?

Select the **Time** and **Temperature** columns in the Go Green spreadsheet by clicking and dragging on them, then choose **Insert > Chart** to open the **Chart Wizard**. Follow the steps on page 3 of **CD Resource 2b – Organise, analyse and chart data** to create and format your chart.

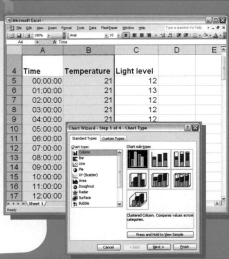

Environmental Tourists

Tutorial 3 Automatic data capture

Go Green are ready to begin their mission to attract more young people to go on their green holidays. They want to put a dynamic display in their shop window that provides up-to-date weather information for some of their European destinations.

By the end of this tutorial you will be able to:

- Create an automatically updatable web query using a spreadsheet
- Recognise when it is important to be able to automatically update data

Step 3.1

Find tabular weather data

Go Green want to display up-to-date weather information for various European cities. One way of doing this is to import data from the internet into a spreadsheet.

Find a website which shows weather data for Europe in **tabular** form. **Tabular** means it is shown in a table. The Met Office website has good tabular data:
www.metoffice.gov.uk/weather/europe/europelatest.html

Latest weather

Location	Weather	Temp	Valid for	Location	Weather	Temp	Valid for
Alicante	☾	7 °C	0600 UTC	Madrid	☾	2 °C	0600 UTC
Amsterdam	☁	4 °C	0600 UTC	Majorca	☁	6 °C	0600 UTC
Athens	☁	5 °C	0600 UTC	Malaga	☾	12 °C	0600 UTC
Barcelona	☾	7 °C	0600 UTC	Malta	☁	15 °C	0600 UTC
Berlin	☁	4 °C	0600 UTC	Milan	FOG	-1 °C	0600 UTC
Bonn	☁ MIST	4 °C	0600 UTC	Moscow	☁	-6 °C	0600 UTC
Bordeaux	FOG	5 °C	0600 UTC	Munich	☁ MIST	3 °C	0600 UTC
Brest	☁	8 °C	0600 UTC	Luxembourg	☁ MIST	3 °C	0600 UTC
Brussels	☁ MIST	4 °C	0600 UTC	Lisbon	☁	11 °C	0600 UTC

Step 3.2

Set up a web query

Open a new spreadsheet document. Click in cell **A1**. Then choose **Data > Import External Data > New Web Query**.

You are going to take the data from the web page you found and place it in the spreadsheet.

In the dialogue box that opens, enter the URL of the web page you are taking the data from. You can copy and paste this from the address bar on the web page.

Step 3.3

Import data from the web into a spreadsheet

Next, go to the web page you have opened. Yellow arrows highlight all the tables that can be imported. Click on the arrow that points to the table you want to import.

The yellow arrow will change to a green tick ✓ when you choose it. Then select **Import**.

In the next dialogue box that opens, click on **Existing worksheet**, then click **OK**. You will see the message 'Getting data...' at first, which means the data is importing. This will take a few seconds, after which the data will be placed in your spreadsheet.

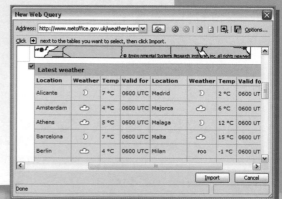

Step 3.4

Update data at chosen intervals

You can tell the spreadsheet to re-import the data from the website at intervals of your choice. This means that if any data has changed, your spreadsheet will be updated with the new data.

Click on a cell in the external data range. The **External Data** toolbar should be displayed. Choose **Data Range Properties**.

Select the **Refresh every** box, and then enter the number of minutes you want to leave between updates (or refreshes). Then choose **OK**.

IMPORTANT: Save your spreadsheet to your folder, and name it **webquery1**. You will be using this later in the module, so you will need to find it easily!

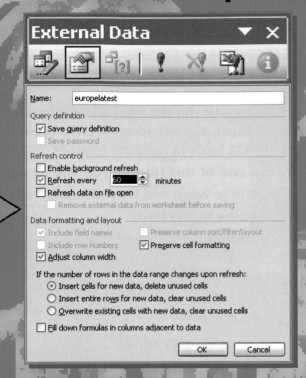

Step 3.5

Examples of data capture systems in industry

Being able to update data automatically is very important in situations where conditions change rapidly.

One example of this is the Stock Exchange, where prices of stocks and shares change from one minute to the next. Having correct information could mean the difference between making or losing a million pounds!

Other examples include traffic information systems, and patient monitoring systems in hospitals.

Step 3.6

Advantages and disadvantages of data capture methods

You now know how to log data using sensors, and how to create an updatable web query using a spreadsheet. These are both types of **data capture**. But are there any downsides to these kinds of information gathering?

Open **CD Resource 3a – Data capture methods** and write down advantages and disadvantages of each method of data capture listed.

Environmental Tourists

Tutorial 6 Creating a presentation

Go Green are attracting quite a lot of passing trade since you created their window display! But they want to reach a wider audience. They have asked you to create a presentation for their new website. The presentation has to explain the importance of green holidays, and include up-to-date information about the holidays they are offering.

By the end of this tutorial you will be able to:
- Plan content and layout of a presentation for a specific purpose
- Create a master slide in a presentation document

Step 6.1

Read and understand a brief

Read the email brief from The Go Green Travel Company on **CD Resource 6a**. This tells you the main things that you need to include.

Use **CD Resource 6b – Presentation planning sheet** to plan the content each slide **must** have, and what each **could** have. For example, contact information is a 'must have', music or sounds are 'could haves'. Make sure your plan is very clear, so that someone else can follow it.

Slide 1	
Must have:	**Title and subtitle** **Picture** **Date and time**
Could have:	**Sound – bubbling water or gentle music**

Step 6.2

Create a presentation from another person's plan

Swap seats with the person sitting next to you. Follow your partner's plan to create the basic presentation they have planned. They will do the same for yours.

In industry, a designer may have to pass over a design for someone else to implement. So it is important to create clear and understandable plans and designs.

Step 6.3

Edit slide master styles

The **slide master** allows you to set styles, fonts and a background that will appear on every slide in your presentation.

To go to the slide master, choose **View > Master > Slide Master**. To return to your presentation, choose **View > Normal**.

Decide what font, size, style and colour you want to use at each level. Select each level to change individual styles, or click on each text box separately and choose the font you want to use for all the text in that box.

Step 6.4

Place a background image on the slide master

If you place a background image on the slide master, the file size will be smaller. This is especially important for use on the internet.

Choose **Insert > Picture > From File** and find a suitable image, or copy and paste an image on to the slide. Then resize the image to fit.

Right-click on the picture and choose **Order > Send to Back** to bring the master text boxes into view again.

Step 6.5

Change saved styles

If you decide you want to change a font or colour, you should usually make changes on the slide master.

Sometimes you will need to change a colour, font size or even the background image. Things that looked good on the slide master may not work when you have a lot of text on a slide.

NOTE: Any changes you make to individual slides will override the slide master styles.

Step 6.6

Automatically update the date and time

To add the date and time to each slide on your presentation, choose **View > Header and Footer**. In the **Date and time** section, click on **Update automatically**, then choose the format you want from the dropdown menu. You can choose to show just the date, or the date and time.

Click **Apply to All**. The correct date and time will now appear at the bottom left-hand side of each slide.

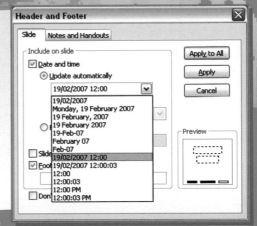

Step 6.7

Prepare slides for adding more content

In the next tutorial, you will be adding more content to your presentation. Make sure that you have three slides with space for adding information about green issues, and updatable weather information on holiday destinations, as described in your brief.

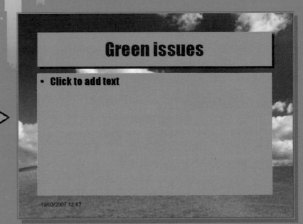

Environmental Tourists

Tutorial 7 Adding content to a presentation

Go Green now want you to add information to your presentation about how tourism can affect the environment, and how people can make alternative, greener holiday choices. They also want you to include the up-to-date weather information for European cities in your presentation.

By the end of this tutorial you will be able to:

- Add a web query to a presentation and set it to update automatically
- Save a presentation as a web page

Step 7.1

Research and add content to a presentation

Open **CD Resource 6c – Green tourism research sheet**. This sheet will help you find key facts about the impact of tourism on the environment, and what people can do to help. Create at least **two slides** to use for this information.

Complete the **research sheet**, either in class or for homework. Then copy and paste the information into your presentation, splitting it across two slides.

NOTE: When you copy and paste text into a presentation, you may need to change the font to match the styles you have already set up.

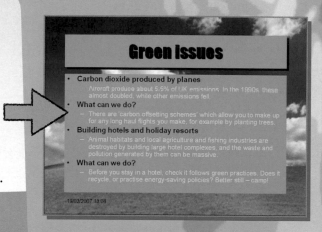

Step 7.2

Add a web query to a presentation (1)

Find and open the web query spreadsheet you created in **Tutorial 3**, named **webquery1**. It should be saved in your folder.

Select all the cells in the table by clicking and dragging on them. Then choose **Edit > Copy**.

Step 7.3

Add a web query to a presentation (2)

Go to the slide in your presentation where you want to place the table, and choose **Edit > Paste Special**.

In the dialogue box that opens, select **Paste**, then choose **Microsoft Office Excel Worksheet Object**.

Click **OK**. The table will be placed in your presentation as an editable and updatable spreadsheet.

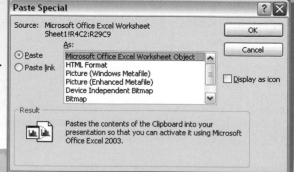

Tutorial 7   Adding content to a presentation

Step 7.4

Format a spreadsheet object

The table may not be very readable, as it will not have a background colour. Right-click on the object to select it, then choose **Format Object > Colour**. Select a contrasting colour for the background.

Enlarge the object if necessary by clicking and dragging on its selection handles.

Step 7.5

Edit a spreadsheet object in a presentation

To edit a spreadsheet object in a presentation, double-click on it. You will see that all the spreadsheet column and row headers appear on the object as shown in the screenshot on the right.

Step 7.6

Set a spreadsheet object to update at chosen intervals

You want the spreadsheet to update so that it shows the most current weather information.

With the spreadsheet open as an editable object, make sure the data is all selected, then right-click on the selected data and choose **Data Range Properties**.

Set the **Refresh Control** to refresh at intervals of your choice.

Now save your presentation as **gogreen_presentation_1**.

Step 7.7

Save a presentation as a web page

Once you have completed your presentation and added all the content, you can save it as a web page. Go to **File > Save as Web Page** and save the presentation to your folder. Name it **gogreen_presentation_web**.

Go Green Holidays presentation_files

Go Green Holidays presentation
HTML Document
3 KB

When you open your folder, you will see that it has saved a folder and a web page, as shown above. Click on the web page, and your presentation will open in your browser window. You should now be able to navigate through the presentation using the menu on the left-hand side of the screen.

Environmental Tourists

Tutorial 8 Evaluating and refining a presentation

Before you show your presentation to the owners of The Go Green Travel Company, you need to evaluate it to make sure that it answers the brief they gave you, and check that it is fit for audience and purpose.

By the end of this tutorial you will be able to:

- Evaluate your work, checking it against the original brief
- Refine and improve your work, making necessary changes and adding enhancements

Step 8.1

Check a presentation against a brief

The first important thing to do is to check your brief, and see if you have done everything it asked you to do.

Open your presentation **gogreen_presentation_1** (not the web version) and a copy of the original brief. Swap seats with a partner and make notes in the **Notes** section at the bottom of each slide to comment on how well they have answered the brief. They should do the same for your presentation. Read their comments, and make at least one of their suggested changes.

Step 8.2

Revise a presentation to address a specific audience

Your presentation is to be aimed at teenagers aged between 13–18 years of age. How could you refine it to make it appeal to this age group? Think about:

Colours – what colours would appeal to young people?
Pictures – cartoons? Photos?
Text – how would you write in a way that appeals to teenagers?
Font – what style of font would be best for this age group?

Text 1:

The carbon emissions from planes taking tourists to exotic, faraway destinations have a devastating effect on the environment.

Text 2:

Tourists take note: long plane journeys are really, really bad news for the environment! This is because of the amount of carbon dioxide and other harmful gases they pump into the air.

Step 8.3

What are hyperlinks?

Another easy way of collecting web-based information quickly is to use **hyperlinks**. A hyperlink is a piece of code that tells the computer to go to a specific web page when clicked on.

Use a search engine to find two good websites with information about tourism and the environment. Try to find websites that would be appealing to teenagers.

Tutorial 8   Evaluating and refining a presentation

Step 8.4

Add a hyperlink to a presentation (1)

Insert a new slide at the end of your presentation and title it 'Web links' or similar.

To add a hyperlink, type in the name of the website and write a sentence below it describing the site, like the example shown on the right.

Then select the name of the website, and right-click on it. Choose **Hyperlink** from the dropdown menu.

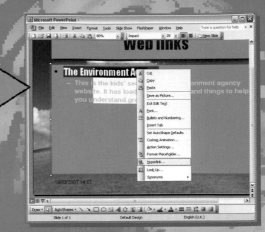

Step 8.5

Add a hyperlink to a presentation (2)

Text to display should show the name of the website – you can leave this as it is.

In the **Address** field, type or paste in the web address.

Click **OK**. You will see that the name of the web page is now underlined, and when you play it as a slide show the link will be active.

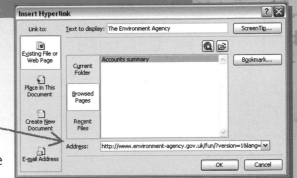

Step 8.6

Annotate your work (1)

The final step is to annotate your work, evaluating it to explain your working processes.

Go to your unit folder and open the following files:

1. Spreadsheet showing chart of logged data (**datalog1**)
2. Spreadsheet showing web query (**webquery1**)

Step 8.7

Annotate your work (2)

Insert text boxes on both your spreadsheets, and use them to explain the following:

1. What does the data in the spreadsheet show?
2. How was data collected and entered into the spreadsheet?
3. How did you organise and analyse the data? (what formulae were used for calculating average, maximum and minimum values and range?)
4. What advantages and/or disadvantages are there to collecting and analysing data in this way?

Environmental Tourists

UNIT

Unit assessment: Getting Grimechester green

Introduction

In the town of Grimechester, an environmental group, Grimestoppers UK, has decided to run a campaign to make people more aware of global warming. They want to give people facts about how bad global warming is and what can be done about it, using temperature data for the UK. They also want to provide charts to show how temperatures have changed over time to show that global warming is a reality.

The problem is, no one at Grimestoppers HQ has a clue where to start, so they have brought you in to help.

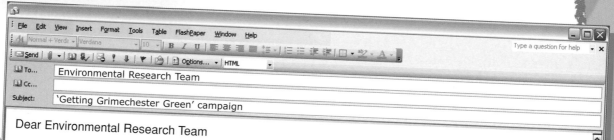

File Edit View Insert Format Tools Table FlashPaper Window Help

Normal + Verde ▾ Verdana ▾ 10 ▾ | **B** *I* U | 歪 枣 彊 畺 | 弍 ▾ | 担 彊 律 悍 | □ ▾ ab2 ▾ A ▾ |

Send | 0 ▾ | 🗎 🗐 | 🗐 ! ↓ | ▼ | 🗐 | 🗐 Options... ▾ | HTML

To...   Environmental Research Team

Cc...

Subject: 'Getting Grimechester Green' campaign

Dear Environmental Research Team

I am writing to ask for your help! We are running a campaign to get grotty old Grimechester greener! We've noticed that Grimechester people don't recycle, use too much energy, and drive to work – even when it's only a five-minute walk! We want to make them aware of what their bad habits are doing to the environment, and how they can get greener.

We have found some local weather data in the public library for the last fifty years and also some data from the 1600s, 1700s and 1800s, and we think that this could be used to show how global warming is happening. We've put the data into four separate worksheets in a spreadsheet, but no one here knows how to use it. Can you help us analyse the data, and make some useful charts?

We have attached a document that outlines exactly what we want you to do.

We are going to produce an information presentation to show to local businesses and schools, showing some of the everyday things that cause damage to the environment (like car exhaust fumes adding to the greenhouse effect), and what people can do to help reduce the damage (like cycling to work). We would like to put the charts that you create into the presentation.

We want you to create a plan for our designer, to show where everything will be placed in the presentation. Write design directions to show what each slide will contain, and notes on any extras like sounds or pictures if you think they will add to the presentation.

Many thanks, we are looking forward to seeing your charts and presentation plans.

Peaches Zappa

Grimestoppers UK
Great Garbage Street
Grimechester
Murkeyside
MY1 8HG
Tel: 0808 112233
Email: campaigndesk@grimestoppers.co.uk

Unit assessment: Getting Grimechester green

Assessment tips:

- Open **CD Resource 9c** and save it as **Unit 8.1 – Data** in your folder **Unit 8.1 – Environmental Tourists**.
- Open **CD Resources 9a** and **9b** and read them carefully. This tells you exactly what Grimestoppers want you to do.
- Think about what the main purpose of the task is. What information do Grimestoppers want to show?
- You don't have to actually design the presentation, but you do need to create a clear and readable plan for the presentation for someone else to follow.

Glossary of key words

Term	Definition	Term	Definition
Analogue	An analogue sensor measures over a continuous range; for example, a mercury thermometer.	**Process**	What a computer does to raw data in order to make it useful and understandable for people.
Analogue to digital converter	A device that converts an analogue value into a digital signal.	**Public information system**	A computerised system that provides information to the general public. For example, a departures board at an airport.
Average	An approximate or levelled value that shows the statistical norm or expected value.	**Refresh**	Update or renew. Used in Excel to mean automatically importing new data to replace old data.
Datalogging	The automatic collection of data over a period of time.	**RSS feed**	A standard way of publishing continuously updated data to a user.
Digital	A digital sensor uses numbers or symbols to represent quantities. Readings are not continuous; they jump between values, for example, a digital watch.	**Sensor**	A device that records physical conditions or stimuli; for example, a thermometer or motion sensor.
GIGO garbage in, garbage out	If the input data is inaccurate, the output data will be too.	**Slide master**	A template in presentation software, used to set styles and add objects, sounds or animations that will appear on all slides in the presentation.
Input	Put data into a computer; for example, by typing on a keyboard, using a sensor or downloading from the internet.	**Trend**	The general direction, either up or down, in which something has been moving; for example, the long-term trend in house prices is upward.
Layered data	A related set of data that can be placed over digital maps so that it can be explored geographically.	**Trendline**	In a chart, a line drawn across the chart which shows the direction or trend.
Output	Data that comes out of a computer after having been processed in some way. This could be a table or chart, or an action such as a door opening.	**Web query**	A function of spreadsheet software that allows you to import data from web pages into a spreadsheet and update it automatically.

Model answer Level 5

To achieve a Level 5 you will need to:

✓ Show understanding of different ways of collecting data automatically

✓ Show that you know the basic differences between analogue and digital sensors

✓ Carry out basic analysis of collected data using a spreadsheet

✓ Critically evaluate your work, and suggest improvements

> This is my chart showing temperature data from the Go Green shop. The data was collected using a sensor.

> I should have chosen a chart type without all the data points showing. I could also make the text bigger and bolder so people can read it easier.

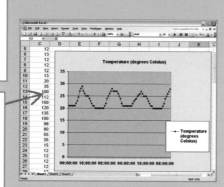

> I used formulae to analyse the data. I found average, maximum and minimum temperatures.
>
> The average temperature in the shop is 23.12 degrees. The formula is =AVERAGE(B5:B89). The maximum is 29 degrees.

Teacher says: *This student has created a useful chart from the sample data file, and his annotation shows that he understands how the data was collected. He has analysed the data using the correct formulae for average, maximum and minimum temperatures, but has not drawn any conclusions from this analysis, or at least, he has not annotated his work to explain this. If he had, he could have achieved a higher level.*

> It was important to make it interesting and useful for tourists. I included pictures and useful information.

> I copied and pasted the data from my web query on to this slide. This is a way of getting data from the web. I made it update every 60 minutes.

> I put the background image and the clipart sun on the slide master. This means that the file size is smaller.

Teacher says: *The student's presentation contains most of the information asked for in the brief – which is very important! He has created a web query, and his annotation shows that he understands what a web query is. The student has also made good use of the slide master to insert images, and he has explained why this is important.*

Model answer Level 6

To achieve a Level 6 you will need to:

✓ Suggest how the presentation of data in information systems is suitable for specific audiences

✓ Use analytical methods to explore patterns in data, and make predictions based on your findings

✓ Present your findings in an appropriate format for your intended audience and purpose

We had to find out if the temperature in the shop was too high. I found that an office should be between 20 and 23 degrees. This shows that the maximum temperature in the shop is too high (29 degrees).

A line chart is good because the data is collected over time. The trend line shows that the average temperature isn't going up or down.

It is easier to see what is happening on the chart than to read the data.

I used spreadsheet formulae to calculate values for average, maximum, minimum and range. The table shows my formulae.

Data analysis and formulae

Average	23.12	=AVERAGE(B5:B89)
Maximum	29.00	=MAX(B5:B89)
Minimum	20.00	=MIN(B5:B89)
Range	9.00	=MAX − MIN

Teacher says: *This student has formatted her chart and added useful data labels – which helps the audience to read the chart. She has explained the purpose of the chart, and drawn some conclusions based on her findings. She also demonstrates in her annotation that she understands why a line chart is a suitable output method for presenting this kind of data.*

The brief asked us to make a presentation to show the ways that people can go on greener holidays.

I included this slide to show the weather in some places in Europe.

I inserted my web query from the Met Office website and set it to update every 60 minutes. This is important because people who are going on holidays will have the most up-to-date weather information.

Teacher says: *The student has created an effective presentation that answers all the points in the brief. She has also explained how she has addressed her audience needs, by including up-to-date weather information.*

8.2 Jump on the Bandwagon!

Tutorial 3 Introduction to Dreamweaver

The band have given you the go-ahead to create the actual website. There are different ways that you can do this, but you are going to use a piece of software called Adobe Dreamweaver.

By the end of this tutorial you will be able to:

- Set up a site folder in Dreamweaver
- Create a layout using a table

Step 3.1

Set up a new site

First, open the web-authoring software, Adobe Dreamweaver.

Choose **Site > Manage Sites**, then in the **Manage Sites** window choose **New > Site**.

Step 3.2

Define your site

This will open the **Site Definition** window. You now need to give your site a name.

Click **Next**, then choose **No, I do not want to use a server technology**.

Then click **Next** again.

Step 3.3

Set up the root folder

You now need to set up a folder where you are going to store your web pages and the **assets** (e.g. images) for your website. This is called the **root folder**.

In **My Documents**, make a folder called **Band Website**. It is important that the root folder is not inside another folder.

Step 3.4

Finish setting up

In the **Site Definition** window choose **None** from the dropdown list. Choose **Done** and then choose **Done** again to finish.

Your site folder is now set up and should appear in the files list on the right-hand side of your screen.

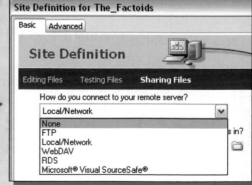

Step 3.5

Open a basic HTML page

Now you have set up your site folder you need to open a new document. You are going to use basic HTML pages for your website.

Choose **File > New**. In the **New Document** window, choose **Basic page** in the left-hand window, and **HTML** in the right.

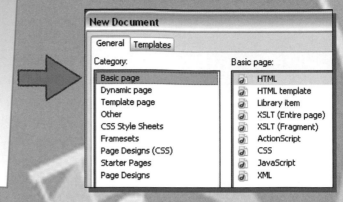

Step 3.6

Create the layout using tables

Now you need to create the layout that you will have on all your pages.

A good way of doing this is to use **tables**. Look at the page layout diagram that you created in **Tutorial 2**. How would you recreate it using tables?

You will need to insert two tables to create the layout shown on the right – Table 1 forms the top banner (one row, one column) and Table 2 forms the side panel and the main content section (one row, two columns).

Step 3.7

Create a table

Click anywhere on the page, and choose **Insert > Table**.

If you are using the layout shown in **Step 3.6**, set your first table to have one row and one column. Then click **OK**. The table will be placed on your page.

Resize the table to fit the page length by clicking and dragging on the corner.

Click underneath the table, and choose **Insert > Table** again. Set your second table to have one row and two columns.

Resize the table to an appropriate size for the page.

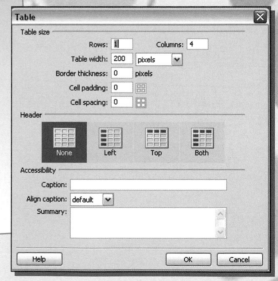

Step 3.8

Save the page as index

When you have created your page layout and resized the tables so you are happy with them, you need to save this page as **index**. Choose **File > Save All**, and save this as **index**. This page will be your homepage.

Jump on the Bandwagon!

Tutorial 4 Creating a homepage and adding images

The band members want a homepage that is exciting and attractive to their fans. They hope that if the site has a really good homepage this will encourage people to explore the site a bit more.

By the end of this tutorial you will be able to:

- Select a colour scheme for the whole website
- Create a homepage for your website

Step 4.1

Add content to your homepage

Open Adobe Dreamweaver and find the **index** page you created in the last tutorial. This is going to be your site homepage.

Click in the top table and type the name of your band. This is going to appear on all the pages in the site.

Type your text for the homepage into the bottom right-hand section as shown on the right.

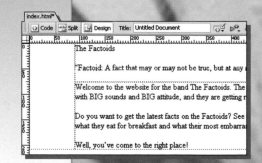

Step 4.2

Format your text

You can now format the font style and size by highlighting the text and clicking on the **Font**, **Style** and **Size** menus located in the **Properties Box** at the bottom of the screen.

To change font colour, click on the **colour picker** icon and choose the colour you want.

Step 4.3

Create a colour scheme

You now need to choose the colour scheme for your site. Remember that all of the pages need to be the same colours, so choose carefully!

Click in the table where you want to add colour. Then click on the **Page Properties** button at the bottom of the screen.

You can now apply colour by clicking on the **Background colour** icon and opening the colour picker. Click **Apply** to add the colour, then choose **OK**. You can leave areas of white, too – you don't have to colour the whole page.

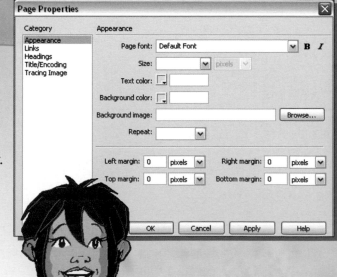

Tutorial 4 | Creating a homepage and adding images

Step 4.4

Create an images folder

All the images you use in your website need to be saved inside the site folder.

To create an images folder, right-click on your site folder. Choose **New Folder** and name this folder **Images**.

Step 4.5

Resize images

If your images are different sizes then you may need to resize them before you put them on your web page. Try to make them quite small, otherwise the page will take too long to load. You can do this using image-editing software such as Microsoft Office Picture Manager, or Adobe® Photoshop®.

Warning: You should **not** resize images after you have placed them on the page in Dreamweaver, because if you put your site on the internet the images won't display properly.

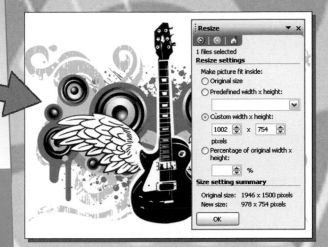

Step 4.6

Place images in tables

Make sure your images are neat and tidy on the page by putting them into tables.

Click underneath your text in the main section of the page. Choose **Insert > Table**.

Set this new table to have one row and as many columns as you have images. Then click **OK**. Click on the corner of the table and drag to resize it on the page.

Step 4.7

Place an image in a table

Once you have placed your table on the page, you need to put an image into each cell of the table.

Click in the first cell and choose **Insert > Image**. Now find the Images folder you created in your site folder, and double-click on the image that you want. The image will appear in your table.

Insert the rest of your images using the same technique.

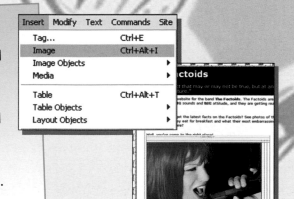

8.2 Jump on the Bandwagon!

Tutorial 5 Creating pages and adding links

The band are very happy with the homepage you have created for them. They now want you to create the remaining pages, and add links between the pages so they can see how the fans will navigate around the site.

By the end of this tutorial you will be able to:
- Use your sitemap diagram to create the rest of the pages
- Set up links allowing the user to move from page to page

Step 5.1

Create new pages in a website

The easiest way to create new pages for your website is to re-save the index page using **Save As**, and rename it each time using the page titles on your sitemap (e.g. news, photos, biography). Do this for every page you want to include in the site.

Using your sitemap to help you, create the rest of the pages for your site. As you save new pages, they will appear in the **File** list on the right-hand side of your screen.

Important: Choose short, descriptive names for each page with **no capitals** and **no spaces**. Use the underscore sign to separate words, for example:

Good: **the_factoids**
Bad: **The Factoids Web Site**

Step 5.2

Add content to web pages

When you have saved all the pages you want in the website, you can start to add your content for each page.

Open one of your other pages that you have just saved (not the index).

Because you used the index page to create all your other pages, you now have the same layout on each page in your site – which is good!

You will also see that all the pages you saved have the content from the index page on them. You can leave the top and left-hand sections as they are, but you will need to delete the content in the main part of the bottom table and add content that is relevant for that page.

Step 5.3

Create links between web pages

Now that you have set up all your pages, you need to create links between them and the homepage. One good way of doing this is by using **Flash Buttons**. Adobe® Flash® is software that allows you to make animated (moving) content. Dreamweaver already contains pre-programmed Flash buttons that you can use.

Open your index page. Click in the left-hand column of the table – this is where you are going to put your links. Then click on the arrow next to the Flash icon on the top menu and choose **Flash Button** from the dropdown menu.

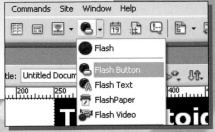

Step 5.4

Add a Flash button (1)

Using the **Style** list, find a button that fits with your colour scheme. You can see what the button will look like in the **Sample** pane.

Note: Some of the buttons are symbols. Make sure that you choose a button that you can add your own words to, not a symbol.

In the **Button text** box, type the name of the page you want to link to, for example, **Gigs**. The buttons have a limited space so your page names should be fairly short!

You now need to link your button to the correct page. On the right-hand side of the **Link** box, click on **Browse**.

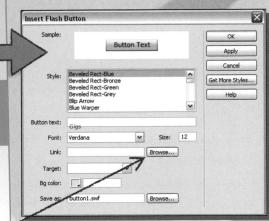

Step 5.5

Add a Flash button (2)

Find the page you want the button to link to in your website folder.

Click on this once to select it. You should see the name of the page appear in the **File name** box. Then click **OK**.

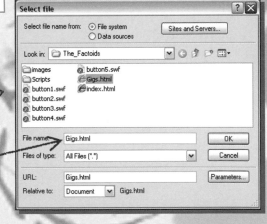

Step 5.6

Add a Flash button (3)

You now need to choose the **Target** for the button.

Using the dropdown menu, select **_parent**, then **Apply** then click **OK**. Save your page, then check your link works by choosing **Preview in Browser**.

Create your other links in the same way. Don't forget to make one called **Home** which links back to the homepage.

Jump on the Bandwagon!

Tutorial 6 Evaluating and improving a website

Your website is nearly complete, and the band have asked you to get some feedback from the target audience to see if they like it. This is very important – if the fans don't like the website they won't revisit it.

By the end of this tutorial you will be able to:

● Evaluate a partner's website

● Make improvements to your site based on a partner's evaluation

● Use criteria to judge the effectiveness of your website

Step 6.1

Evaluate your partner's website

Your band's fans are about your age, so you and your classmates are the best people to evaluate their website! Load your website and open it in the browser. Then swap computers with a partner. Using **CD Resource 6a**, evaluate your partner's website while they do the same for yours.

Some things you might like to think about are listed opposite – you could refer back to **Tutorial 1** in this unit, too.

Using the feedback you have just been given, make the suggested improvements to the website.

EVALUATE!

● **Is it obvious what the website is for, and who it is for?**

● **Can you navigate (find your way) around the site easily?**

● **Do the colours work well together? Is the text easy to read?**

● **Are the images clear and undistorted?**

Step 6.2

Complete your website

Check that all your pages have all the correct content – that means all the text, images and any other content you want to add, for example, animations.

Spellcheck your text and make sure your images are not distorted.

Step 6.3

Test and fix your links

To check your buttons work, you need to save your page and then preview it in your browser. To do this, click on the **Preview in Browser** icon on the top toolbar and select the browser type you are using.

Click on each of the buttons to make sure that they work correctly. Make a note of any that do not, and fix these.

Tutorial 6 Evaluating and improving a website

Step 6.4

Take screenshots of web pages

Open a new word-processing document and choose **File > Page Setup**. Change the **Orientation** to **Landscape**. Click **OK**.

Now take a screenshot of each of your web pages in the browser window using the **Print Screen** key on your keyboard.

Paste each screenshot into the word-processing document using right-click and **Paste**.

You should also include your sitemap and page layout diagrams if you have these electronically.

Step 6.5

Annotate screenshots

As you have done in previous units, you should now add text boxes around the screenshots.

Annotate your screenshots, explaining the choices you have made. You need to explain why you have made the following choices in your website:

- Layout and navigation
- The colours you have used
- The images you have used
- Text and content of each page

Step 6.6

Write an evaluation

Once you have annotated the screenshots, you should write a longer evaluation of the work you have done in this unit.

Create a new page at the end of your document by choosing **Insert > Break > Page Break** and give the page the title 'Website evaluation'.

Use the prompts in the box on the right to help you write your evaluation. You should write one paragraph for each point.

WEBSITE EVALUATION

- **How did you decide what pages to include in your website?**
- **How did you plan the structure of the site and the page layout?**
- **What did you find hard about creating a website? How did you overcome these difficulties?**
- **What would you like to add to your site to make it even better?**

Jump on the Bandwagon!

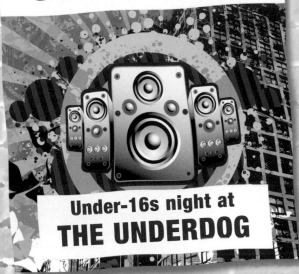

schmoozic

Under-16s night at THE UNDERDOG

Unit assessment
Schmoozic Night

Introduction

Your band website has made you quite a name in the music business, and people are starting to notice you! A nightclub manager has spotted your talent and wants you to create a website for a new youth night he is putting on at his club.

Read the email below which tells you about the night. There is also an attachment which you will need to read before you begin this assessed activity.

File Edit View Insert Format Tools Table FlashPaper Window Help

Type a question for help

To... Web Design Team

Cc...

Subject: Schmoozic Night website

Dear Web Design Team

Keith Cavern, the manager of a local club called The Underdog, has commissioned us to design a website to promote an 'Under-16s' night that he has just started called 'Schmoozic'.

The Under-16s night is every Friday, and it's starting to get really popular, but Mr Cavern wants to promote it more. The club is running four events on a Friday night, including:

• Rhythm and Boogie (disco)
• Drum Master Class
• Karaoke Chaos!
• Schmoozic Young Bands Competition

Your website will have to look really good to attract young people aged 13–16 to the club, and also tell them about each of the events listed above. Additionally, it will need to contain basic information about the club, where it is, the telephone number and how much it costs to get in.

Read the instructions your teacher gives you carefully before you start.

Good luck,
Will Webber
Head of Web Design

Assessment tips:

- Load and set up a new root folder in Dreamweaver. Save it as **Unit 8.2 Unit assessment** in your folder **Unit 8.2 – Bandwagon**.
- Read the instructions in the attachment (**CD Resource 7b**) carefully.
- Draw a sitemap and page layout so you can refer to this while you are building the site.
- Experiment with different colours to see which colours work well and which do not.
- Choose your font style and size carefully.
- The text should be easy to read and stand out well against your chosen background colour.
- Only use images that are saved in the **Images** folder in the website folder.

Glossary of key words

Flash	A program that can be used to develop animations and graphics for websites.	**Layout**	The arrangement of objects such as text and images on a page.
Flash button	A button that has been created in Flash that can be used on a website.	**Navigation**	The way in which we move around within a website or the web.
Homepage	The first page a visitor will come to when visiting a website. It acts as an index page for the site and is usually saved as **index**.	**Rollover/ mouseover**	A graphic on a web page that changes in some way when the mouse passes over it. It usually signifies a link.
HTML (hypertext mark-up language)	A computer programming language that is used to create web pages.	**Root folder**	The folder in which everything that is included in a website must be saved, including images.
		Sitemap	A diagram that shows the structure of a website and how all the pages link.
Hyperlink (often shortened to 'link')	A specific word, object or image which can be clicked on to move to another page or placed in a website. This is used to link pages together in a website.	**Table**	A set of data arranged in rows and columns.
		Web page	A single page, usually part of a collection of web pages called a website.
Index	The first page of a website which appears to the user in the browser. It is usually the site's homepage.	**Website**	A collection of linked web pages.

Model answer Level 5

To achieve a Level 5 you will need to:

✔ Create a clear plan of your structure and layout, showing links

✔ Create between one and three linked web pages which contain some suitable graphics

✔ Add appropriate colour to background, font and text

✔ Add appropriate images and text, showing an appreciation of audience and purpose

First I made a plan of the structure for the website. I put in each page and also put lines showing links.

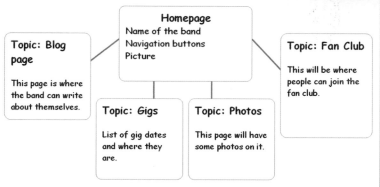

Homepage
Name of the band
Navigation buttons
Picture

Topic: Blog page

This page is where the band can write about themselves.

Topic: Fan Club

This will be where people can join the fan club.

Topic: Gigs

List of gig dates and where they are.

Topic: Photos

This page will have some photos on it.

Teacher says: *This student has produced a clear and useable plan for his website, which shows page topics and links.*

I put my links on the left side on all pages. This means people can find them easily. I checked them to make sure they work.

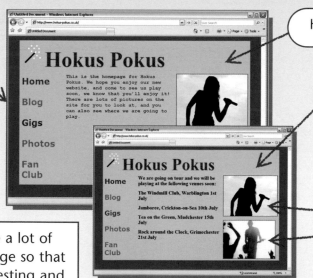

Homepage

Gigs page

I used two pictures to show the band playing. I think I should have chosen more pictures because I used the same ones on all the pages.

I have used quite a lot of colours on each page so that the site looks interesting and appeals to teenagers.

Teacher says: *The site is clearly laid out and easy to navigate. The colours work nicely together, but could have been limited to two or three. The student should have made the fonts on both pages the same style and colour for consistency.*

Teacher says: *The images are appropriate, but could have been more varied. The student recognises this in his annotation, though. Annotation is good, and gives at least one way in which the student thought about the audience in his choice of colour.*

Model answer Level 6

To achieve a Level 6 you will need to:

✓ Choose colours, images and text that show a clear awareness of audience and purpose

✓ Use some of the more advanced functions of a web-authoring software package

✓ Refine your website, making sure that images, buttons and text are tidy and aligned

✓ Evaluate your website and suggest improvements

This plan shows the pages in my website and how they are linked. I would like to add more pages at some point.

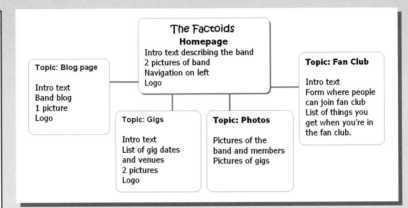

The Factoids
Homepage
Intro text describing the band
2 pictures of band
Navigation on left
Logo

Topic: Blog page

Intro text
Band blog
1 picture
Logo

Topic: Gigs

Intro text
List of gig dates
and venues
2 pictures
Logo

Topic: Photos

Pictures of the
band and members
Pictures of gigs

Topic: Fan Club

Intro text
Form where people
can join fan club
List of things you
get when you're in
the fan club.

I looked at a real band's website to get some ideas for what pages band websites should have.

Teacher says: *This student's plan is clear to read, and lists in some detail what she is planning to include on each page.*

I made the colours quite dark because the music my band plays is moody and angry! I think it is a bit too dark though. I would make the title a bit brighter so you can see it better.

I chose an attractive font for the title. All the other text is Arial. I made this the same on all pages.

There is a lot of blank space on some pages so I would improve this by adding something here, maybe another picture.

I made everything line up on the page by using tables. That means pictures and buttons look tidy.

Teacher says: *This site is a high Level 6. The student has created a website that immediately looks professional and appealing. Images are clear and work well with the background greys. The student has refined their work to line up images, etc. This instantly transforms a good website into an excellent one!*

Teacher says: *Annotation is good and explains the student's ideas well. The student can see where she is not happy with the site, and how she would like to improve it.*

Information Superhighway

Unit introduction

In this unit you are going to develop your information-seeking skills by carrying out research into current issues and debates such as animal testing and Third World debt.

The internet is a great place to find information quickly, but it is important to be able to recognise and select information that is reliable, accurate and unbiased.

You will then produce a learning aid for younger students that helps them to understand one of the issues you have researched.

Unit learning objectives

We are learning to:

- Find information for a particular purpose, explaining why we have chosen it
- Consider the source of the information we find
- Use advanced searches to make finding information more efficient
- Produce a presentation which takes account of audience needs
- Evaluate information for reliability, validity and bias

Unit preparation

1. You will need to set up a folder in your area and name it **Unit 8.3 – Information Superhighway**.

2. You will need to know how to load an internet browser such as **Internet Explorer**.

3. You should know how to use a search engine to find a website.

Start thinking about ...

Fact or opinion?

One of the most important things to remember in this unit is to always question the information you find, and to consider whether a statement is **fact** or **opinion**.

Remember – anyone can create a website. The author could have very strong opinions, be trying to sell something, or even just be making things up for fun, like in hoax websites.

Look at the statements opposite. Are they facts, or opinions? How do you know? If they are facts, are they correct? How could you check them?

Eating a lot of red meat can cause heart disease.

It is not right to experiment on animals.

England is a great place to live.

Islam has the most followers of all the religions in the world.

Vincent van Gogh painted the painting Sunflowers.

Vincent van Gogh was the greatest artist who ever lived.

Step 1.1

What is a URL?
URL means **uniform resource locator**. This is the address of the website and will be unique. There are billions of websites on the World Wide Web, so it is important to type in the URL correctly.

Remember that the URL does not tell you everything – it only gives an indication of whether a site is likely to give you the information you need.

Domain name

Originates in the UK

www.medicalmouse.org.uk

Domain type – this example tells us the site is probably run by a not-for-profit organisation

Step 1.2

Domain types and country types
A URL can tell us quite a lot about the website and its author. The **domain type** can tell you something about who made the website or who it belongs to. The **country type** tells us the country in which it was made.

The table on the right contains some useful reminders of what URL endings can tell us.

Note: The domain type **.com** is mainly used by American companies. However, many other companies also use this, so it is hard to tell without visiting the site where a .com website originates.

.co	Company	.org	Organisation (can be a charity)
.ac	Academic (universities)	.ed	Education (university or college)
.com	International company	.fr	Originates in France
.sch	School	.uk	Originates in the United Kingdom
.net	Network	.es	Originates in Spain
.gov	Government site	.us	Originates in the United States

Step 1.3

Distinguish between fact and opinion
Before using information you should always begin by deciding whether it is **fact** or **opinion**. Remember: a fact can be scientifically proven. An opinion is the way somebody feels – there may be facts to support these feelings, but do not confuse this with a fact.

95% of drugs passed by animal tests are immediately thrown away as useless or dangerous to humans.

I can't stand animal testing, it's really horrible and we shouldn't do it.

Step 1.4

Identify reliability and bias
You also need to decide whether the information you find is **reliable** (trustworthy). You can get an idea of how reliable a website is by looking at its URL, its author or organisation and the design of the site itself. Does it have logos? Does it look like an official site? Is it a commercial site (selling you something)? Is it a scientific or educational site?

Bias means when the author has a very strong opinion on a subject, which means you only get one side of the story. The information could still be useful, but you will also need to look elsewhere for websites that consider the other side of the argument.

Kids who get more pocket money get higher marks in school.

Yes, but you're biased, aren't you?

Information Superhighway

Tutorial 2 Finding relevant information

In this tutorial you will focus on developing your information-seeking skills. You will also consider the quality of the information you find.

By the end of this tutorial you will be able to:

- Search for key words within a document
- Develop more advanced search skills using 'Boolean connectors' (**AND/OR/NOT**)
- Assess information for bias and reliability
- Consider other potential sources of information

Step 2.1

Use the Find function in Microsoft Word

You can search for specific words within documents. The number of times these words occur will give us an indication of the type of information the document contains. In later versions of Microsoft Office, the **Find** box can also be used to highlight the key words, making it easier to spot them.

To search for key words, choose **Edit > Find**. Type the word you are searching for into the **Find what** box, then click on **Find Next**.

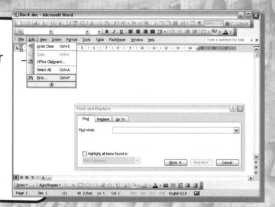

Step 2.2

Find key words in a document

Open **CD Resource 2b – Animal testing fact sheet** and follow the instructions for Activity 1, which ask you to search for specific words in an article on animal testing.

Activity 2 asks you to suggest some other key words. Try to think of words with similar meanings to the ones you have used (these are called synonyms). Can you think of a synonym for 'testing'?

Tip: You can do a similar thing with web pages. When you are on the web page, choose **Edit > Find on this Page**. This will bring up the **Find** box. Type in the word you are searching for, and click on **Next**.

Synonyms are words with similar meaning …

Scared
Alarmed
Fearful
Frightened
Petrified
Terrified

Step 2.3

Search engines

A search engine like Google also works on the basis of key words. When you type a word into the search box, the search engine looks for all the websites that contain the words you have entered. This is why it is important to decide which words are likely to be in the type of document you want to find.

Tutorial 2 Finding relevant information

Boolean connectors

Boolean connectors are words that you can use to help you either narrow or widen a search. The Boolean connectors you are going to use are **AND**, **OR** and **NOT**.

AND searches for pages that contain all of the words. For example, typing **cat AND dog** in the search box tells the search engine to find web pages that contain both these words. (Most search engines do this automatically.)

NOT will narrow a search by adding a restriction. For example, typing **cat NOT dog** is telling the search engine to find web pages containing the word cat but throw away those that also contain the word dog. (In Google, in order to do a 'NOT' search, you must use a minus sign. For example, **cat -dog**.)

OR widens the search. For example, typing **cat OR dog** is telling the search engine to find examples of web pages that contain either of these words, or both.

Step 2.5

Use Boolean connectors

You are now going to use Boolean connectors with the key words you identified in **Step 2.2** to find useful information on animal testing.

You need to search the internet to find some more information about animal testing. You need to make use of all three connectors **AND**, **NOT** and **OR** in the searches you carry out.

Remember: If you use Google, AND is automatically placed between the words, so you don't need to type this in.

Google   Web   Images   Groups

animal OR testing

Search: ⦿ the web ○ pa

Web

Animal
Design-led, rider-refined sports brand making accessorie
Includes dealer listing and online catalogue with prices.
www.**animal**.co.uk/ - 2k - Cached - Similar pages

Step 2.6

Other sources of information

The internet is a very useful source of information. It allows you to search through lots of material very quickly and easily.

There are, however, many other sources of information. Some other places information could be gathered from include:
- **CD ROMs**
- **Books**
- **Magazines**
- **Leaflets**

Can you think of any more?

Imagine having your body left to science ... while you're still in it.

PeTA

Information Superhighway

UNIT

Tutorial 3 Refining search skills

In this tutorial you will work to refine your search skills and begin to use more advanced methods of searching for information. You will also begin to investigate a new topic, Third World debt.

By the end of this tutorial you will be able to:

- Understand the meaning of validity
- Independently use some advanced search techniques
- Understand what makes information reliable
- Start to use different sources of information in your research

Step 3.1

Validity of information

Valid information is information that can be backed up in some way and that is relevant to the point you are trying to make. Some key points to think about are:

- Is the information up-to-date? If you are reading a report dated 2001, it is likely that the information is no longer valid.
- Who has written the information? Is it an official source, or a personal website? If it is one person's website, you should check other sources to see if they say the same thing.
- What country does the information refer to? If you are taking information from a website based in the USA, the information won't necessarily be relevant to the UK.

Step 3.2

Relevance of search results

When you use an internet search engine it usually returns thousands (sometimes millions!) of results. This can make it difficult to decide which results are likely to be the most relevant.

Step 3.3

Advanced Search options

There are a range of **Advanced Search** options that can be used with the Google search engine.

To access these options, choose **Advanced Search**, which is located next to the **Search** box from the standard Google search page.

You will see on this screen a range of boxes and dropdown menus that you can use to narrow down your search. For example, you can tell Google to find only web pages which have been updated in the last three months, or which include an exact phrase.

Step 3.4

Use Advanced Search options

Find and open **CD Resource 3b – Third World debt worksheet** and complete Activity 1, which is a timed practice activity using the Google Advanced Search facility.

You have 10 minutes to complete the activity. In this time you need to use the Advanced Search options to narrow down your search results as much as possible.

You can also use the Boolean connectors **AND**, **OR** and **NOT** if you are feeling adventurous!

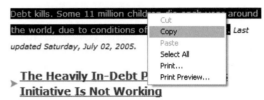

Step 3.5

Select, copy and paste relevant information for a task

Now look at Activity 2 on the same sheet. In this activity you have to collect some information. Once again you will have 10 minutes to search for information that gives answers to the questions on the worksheet.

Copy and paste relevant information into the worksheet. To do this, select the information you want, then choose **Edit > Copy**. Then go to the worksheet, click on the page where you want to paste the information and choose **Edit > Paste**.

Tip: You can right-click and choose **Copy**, then right-click and **Paste** if you prefer this method (PC users only).

Debt kills. Some 11 million children die each year around the world, due to conditions of ... Last updated Saturday, July 02, 2005.

> **The Heavily In-Debt P___
> Initiative Is Not Working**

The Heavily In-debt Poor Countries (HIPC) initiative set up in 1996 by the rich nations through the IMF and World Bank calls for the reduction of external debt for the poorest countries through write-offs by official donors.

Cut
Copy
Paste
Select All
Print...
Print Preview...

Step 3.6

You should now have enough information to answer all the questions on the Team quiz sheet (**CD Resource 3c**). Rewrite the information if necessary so that you answer the questions you are being asked.

Note: You should always rewrite information you find **in your own words**. If you copy information word-for-word, you must always **cite your source** (say where it came from) otherwise you are in danger of breaking copyright laws.

Original

Debt kills. Some 11 million children die each year around the world, due to conditions of poverty and debt.

Rewritten

Poverty caused by Third World debt kills around 11 million children each year.

Information Superhighway

UNIT

Tutorial 4 Project planning and research

In this tutorial you will focus on completing the first stages of a challenge project. You are going to produce a learning aid for Year 7 students. The email below gives you more detail about what you have to do.

By the end of this tutorial you will be able to:

- Plan the structure and content of a project
- Find and select information that is relevant and reliable
- Review the information you find in terms of validity and bias

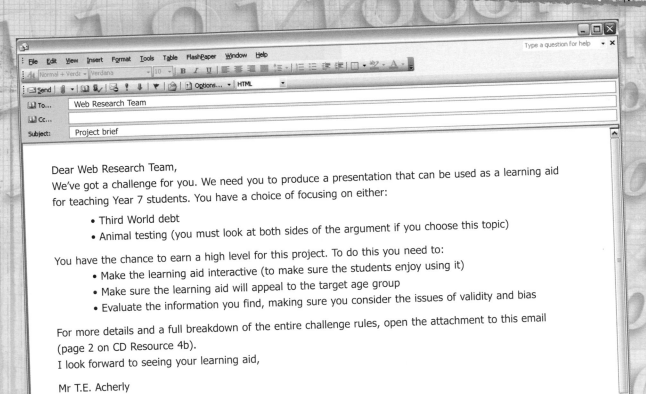

Dear Web Research Team,

We've got a challenge for you. We need you to produce a presentation that can be used as a learning aid for teaching Year 7 students. You have a choice of focusing on either:

- Third World debt
- Animal testing (you must look at both sides of the argument if you choose this topic)

You have the chance to earn a high level for this project. To do this you need to:

- Make the learning aid interactive (to make sure the students enjoy using it)
- Make sure the learning aid will appeal to the target age group
- Evaluate the information you find, making sure you consider the issues of validity and bias

For more details and a full breakdown of the entire challenge rules, open the attachment to this email (page 2 on CD Resource 4b).

I look forward to seeing your learning aid,

Mr T.E. Acherly
E-Learning Manager
World Citizens Learning Tools Ltd

Step 4.1

Plan a project

The first task you need to undertake is to plan the outline of your presentation.

You should now complete **CD Resource 4c – Project planning sheet**.

1. Decide which topic you want to research.
2. Decide on a good title for the presentation.
3. Plan each slide you are going to include and give each a heading.

Tip: You may find that you need to change the content or structure of your slides as you find out more about the subject.

Tutorial 4 Project planning and research

Step 4.2

Gather and organise information

Open a new word-processing document, and copy and paste the slide headings you created in **Step 4.1** into it. Leave spaces underneath each heading – this is where you are going to paste information you find.

When you find a piece of information you want to use, copy and paste it into your document under the most appropriate heading.

Tip: You should only copy the key points you want to use into your word-processed document.

Step 4.3

Cite your sources

When you have copied and pasted your information, you must add the URL to show where the information came from.

This is important for three reasons: firstly, so that you can find the website again! Secondly, so that it is clear that you have not just made up the information. Finally, it is important to give credit to the author of the information so that you are not breaking copyright laws.

Step 4.4

Rewrite your information

When you think you have found enough information for each slide, you should rewrite it in your own words. Think about your audience too – you are writing for Year 7 students, so the information must be clear and understandable for that age group.

Tip: In recent versions of Microsoft Word, you can right-click on words to get a list of synonyms.

Step 4.5

Review your information

Once you are happy with the content and the structure of your project, you should review the information in each section to explain why you think it is suitable for use. Some things to think about are listed opposite.

Write five sentences at the end of your word-processed document that answer the questions shown on the right.

Make the sentences into bullet points, or number them 1–5.

What things do we test on animals?

Cosmetics and medicine are tested on animals although it is illegal in the UK to test cosmetics on animals.

Do we need to test on animals?

What animals are tested on?

Third World debt countries

Some of the countries with massive debt include Ethiopia, Rwanda and Nigeria ...

(**www.questionsandanswers.com**)

Problems associated with Third World debt

What can be done about it?

Original: Animal rights extremists have conducted a sustained campaign of harassment and **intimidation** against the animal research industry, including targeting people at home and in their communities.

Rewritten: Animal rights extremists sometimes make **threats** to people who work in the animal testing industry.

Review points:

- Is it giving facts or opinions?
- Is it valid information (up-to-date, relevant and reliable)?
- Is it biased one way or another?
- If it is biased, have you included information that gives the other side of the argument?
- Is it suitable for the audience it is aimed at?

UNIT

Tutorial 5 Designing a presentation

In this tutorial you will be producing your learning aid, using presentation software. You should already have the text you are going to use for each slide. If you feel really confident with web-authoring software, you could create a website instead (refer to **Unit 8.2 – Jump on the Bandwagon!**). However, you only have limited time for this task, so only do that if you know you can do it in the time available!

By the end of this tutorial you will be able to:

- Create new slides and add titles and text

- Choose a good colour scheme for the learning aid

- Add age appropriate, relevant images to illustrate points you make in the text

- Add animation appropriately

Step 5.1

Create a new presentation and add text
Open your presentation software (Microsoft PowerPoint or similar) and create however many slides you have planned.

Then open your word-processed document containing the text you worked on in the last tutorial. Copy and paste the titles from each section on to the correct slide in your presentation.

Finally, copy and paste your text on to each slide. Make sure you have put everything in the right place, then save your presentation to your folder.

Step 5.2

Choose a font and background colour
You need to make your learning aid appealing to Year 7 students. Colour is an important part of both presentations and websites.

Your audience will like bright colours, but you should not use too many colours or they will be distracted from the text. Font and background colours should be high contrast (dark on light, or light on dark).

Look at the slide shown opposite. Why do you think it is appealing to 11- to 12-year-old students?

Tutorial 5 Designing a presentation

Add images to illustrate points

Images are especially important in a presentation for children. Don't include images that are too upsetting – remember, your audience are only 11–12 years old.

The images should illustrate points you are making. For example, if you have a slide that outlines the bad things about animal testing, you could include a picture of an animal in a cage. However, if you have a slide that talks about the benefits of animal testing it would be better to use an image that shows medicines, or a patient in a hospital.

You could also use **charts** or **graphs** if there are a lot of statistics in the subject you are researching. It is often hard for people (particularly children) to imagine large numbers or trends unless they are shown in a chart.

Step 5.4

Add animation to a presentation

Sometimes it is useful to add animation to text. This allows you to bring in points you are making one at a time, so that the audience does not have too much to read all in one go.

To animate text, click on the text box you want to animate, then choose **Slide Show > Animation Schemes**. This will bring up a list of different animation effects; for example, **Appear** or **Faded wipe**. Choose one of these, and then play your slide show by selecting the **Slide Show** icon 🖵 in the bottom left-hand corner of your screen.

You will need to click on the slide to start the animation. Experiment with different effects until you find one you like.

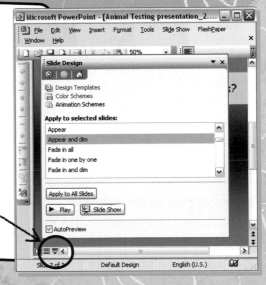

Step 5.5

Slide transitions

You can change the way in which one slide changes to the next by choosing **Slide Show > Slide Transition**. This will open a list of effects. Try a few by clicking on them. You will see a preview of each appear on your slide.

Tip: Animation should be used very sparingly, and only where it is useful; for example, if you have a lot of points on one slide. Be careful with sound effects, too, particularly if you have already included a sound on the slide!

Tutorial 6 Evaluating and revising a presentation

Your learning aid should now be nearly complete, and contain all your text, images, colour scheme and even maybe some animation. In this tutorial you are going to review the work you have done by looking back at the project brief, and making sure that you have answered each point.

Then you can make some final adjustments before you present your work to an audience.

By the end of this tutorial you will be able to:

● Evaluate your work, referring to the project brief

● Make final adjustments to a presentation

● Present your work to an audience

TODAY WE ARE LEARNING?

Step 6.1

Project debriefing

The best way to see if your work is really up to scratch is to look back at the brief you were given at the start of the project.

Read each point on the brief and look at your presentation. Have you done everything the brief asked you to? You can find this on **CD Resource 6b – Project debrief sheet**.

Tick the boxes you think you have answered. If you're not sure, ask a classmate to look at your work and give you their opinion.

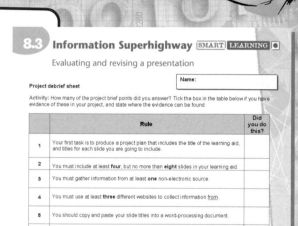

8.3 Information Superhighway [SMART] [LEARNING] ●

Evaluating and revising a presentation

Project debrief sheet

Name:

Activity: How many of the project brief points did you answer? Tick the box in the table below if you have evidence of these in your project, and state where the evidence can be found.

	Rule	Did you do this?
1	Your first task is to produce a project plan that includes the title of the learning aid, and titles for each slide you are going to include.	
2	You must include at least **four**, but no more than **eight** slides in your learning aid.	
3	You must gather information from at least **one** non-electronic source.	
4	You must use at least **three** different websites to collect information from.	
5	You should copy and paste your slide titles into a word-processing document.	
6	You should type, or copy and paste information you want to use into a word-processing document under the relevant slide title.	

Step 6.2

Revise your presentation

If you found anything on the Project debrief sheet that you have not included in your presentation, you should now try to correct this to improve the work you have done.

Even if you answered ALL the points, there may still be improvements you can make. For example:

● Add a short quiz at the end of the presentation, testing students on the information you included.

● Tidy up slides – align textboxes and images, make improvements to font sizes or styles.

● Add enhancements; for example, drop shadows to images.

Quiz time!

• Name 3 products that are tested on animals!
• Give one reason why we should test on animals
• Give one reason why we shouldn't test on animals

Step 6.3

Evaluate your work

Once you are happy with your presentation, print out a copy of **CD Resource 6c – Student evaluation sheet**. Complete the sheet to explain what you did at each stage of the project, and why you did it.

Tutorial 6 Evaluating and revising a presentation

Step 6.4

Test your learning aid on an audience

The whole point of a presentation is that it is designed to be seen by an audience. You have designed your learning aid to be shown to Year 7 students, so ideally you should try to show it to them.

You could either show it to a small group of students around a computer screen, or to a whole class of willing learners on an interactive whiteboard or projector!

Step 6.5

Print handouts to use when presenting

If you are going to present to a class, you will need to stand by the screen and click through the slides yourself, talking through each slide as it appears. You should print out your presentation as handouts and use these to talk about each slide.

To print out slides as handouts, choose **File > Print**. Then go to the **Print what** dropdown menu and choose **Handouts**. On the **Slides per page** dropdown menu, choose how many slides you want to appear on each page (four is a good number). Then click **OK**.

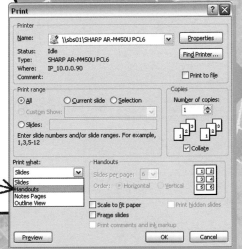

Step 6.6

Get some audience participation

You could add a few notes on to your handouts if you like, so you have got a few things up your sleeve to get the audience thinking.

For example, why not ask the audience a question like, 'Roughly how much do you think Third World debt comes to in total?' But remember, *you* have to know the answer!

Step 6.7

Present your learning aid!

Open your presentation and click on the **Slide Show** icon 🖵 in the bottom left-hand corner of your screen to show the slide show. If you have included animation, this will only appear when you play the slide show. Play your show (don't forget to ask your questions and add information!).

At the end of the presentation, ask the students to give you some comments. Did they enjoy it? Did they learn anything they didn't know before? Is there anything they would like to know that wasn't included?

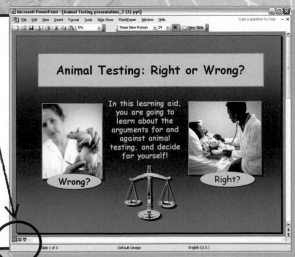

UNIT

Unit assessment Celebrities – are they public property?

Introduction

The Daily Bizarre newspaper has approached you to carry out some research into how the press deals with celebrities. There have been complaints that the press invades celebrities' private lives too much. But the newspaper thinks that there is another side to the story! The Editor has sent you the email below, which outlines what you have to do.

File   Edit   View   Insert   Format   Tools   Table   FlashPaper   Window   Help

Normal + Verda ▾ Verdana   ▾ 10 ▾   B *I* U | ≡ ≡ ≡ ≡ ≣ ▾ | ≔ ≔ ≇ ≇ | □ ▾ ✎ ▾ A ▾

Send 📎 ▾ 📭 🐎 | 🖃 ! ↓ | ▾ | 🖼 | ⋮ Options... ▾ | HTML   ▾

To...	Web Research Team
Cc...	
Subject:	Celebrities – are they public property?

Dear Web Research Team,

I am writing to ask you to do some research for us, investigating the way in which the press handles celebrities. Some celebrities have complained that we invade their private lives, and that we should leave them alone. On the other hand, some celebrities like to have lots of publicity. And we as the press have a duty to report what's happening in the world.

1. We would like you to produce a **plan** and **one sample slide or page** for either a short PowerPoint presentation or a website, aimed at teenagers aged 15–16. Your research should focus on the following question: **Are celebrities entitled to a private life?**

2. First you should create your slide or page titles and type these into a word-processing document. If you decide to make a website, you should create a sitemap. You can find some websites to help you create these if you like.

3. You then need to copy and paste any information you want to use under the relevant title. Make sure that you include the URL of the site where you found it.

4. You should then review the information you find in terms of whether it is:
   - Fact or opinion
   - Valid (up-to-date, UK-based, reliable source?)
   - Biased (does the author hold a strong opinion one way or the other?)

5. Finally, you should rewrite your information so that it is suitable for a teenage audience.

Good luck, and we look forward to seeing your final plan and sample slide or page.

Bert 'No Pressure' Bailey
Senior Editor
The Daily Bizarre

Unit assessment Celebrities – are they public property?

Glossary of key words

Bias	A tendency to support or oppose a particular person or thing in an unfair way by allowing personal opinions to influence your judgement.	**Opinion**	A thought or belief about something or someone, not necessarily backed up by evidence.
Boolean connector	Connecting words that can be used with key words in a search to refine it, for example: AND, OR, NOT. Search engines usually insert AND automatically between search terms.	**Reliable**	Dependable or trustworthy.
Domain name	Name of a website owned by a company or individual. Domain names always have two or more parts, separated by dots. For example, in the URL www.bbc.co.uk, bbc.co.uk is the domain name.	**Search engine**	A program which allows you to search for key words on web pages. Commonly used search engines are Google, Alta Vista, MSN, Lycos and Yahoo.
Fact	Something that is known to have happened or to exist, especially something for which proof exists.	**URL (Uniform Resource Locator)**	Web address. The URL contains the location of a web page or resource on the internet, which may be the homepage or any other page in the website.
HTTP (Hypertext Transfer Protocol)	The set of rules enabling computers to read web pages ('protocol' means 'rules'). This always comes at the beginning of a URL.	**Valid**	Coming from a reliable or official source, and relevant in terms of time and location.

Model answer Level 5

To achieve a Level 5 you will need to:

✓ Select suitable key words to search on, and use some advanced search features

✓ Use electronic sources, and at least one non-electronic source when researching a topic

✓ Show a clear awareness of your audience and design your presentation to suit them

✓ Assess the information you find in terms of validity, reliability and bias

I used a search engine and found some good websites with information. I used wikipedia for a lot of information.

The plan looks a bit messy. I would improve it by making it one font.

Animal testing presentation
Research sheet

Slide 1 Animal testing
This slide is the title slide. It will have a picture and an introduction.

Slide 2 What is animal testing about?

Animal testing is the use of non-human animals in experiments. These may be for the purpose of testing certain substances to determine their effect on humans, or to test medical or psychological hypotheses.
This information is from wikipedia website.
http://en.wikipedia.org/wiki/Animal_testing
I think this is a fact, not opinion. wikipedia is an online encyclopaedia that seems to be a reliable source.

Slide 3 – What animals are used?

Fruit fly
nematodes
rodents like guinea pigs, hamsters, gerbils, rats and mice
fishes and frogs
dogs and monkeys
I got this information from wikipedia.

I copied and pasted the information into my document and also the URL. I could then paste it into my presentation.

Teacher says:
The student has made some attempts to comment on reliability, but she could have commented more on the websites that she used (anyone can post an article on Wikipedia, for example).

Teacher says: *This student has completed a satisfactory research sheet, although it could have been tidied up and formatted to be easier to read – even plans must be neat! The student has recognised in her annotation that she needs to improve this.*

My presentation has a lot of colours to appeal to younger students. I also put in lots of pictures of animals to make it interesting.

What animals are used?

Some animals used in animal testing are:

- **Fruit fly**
- **Nematodes (roundworms)**
- **rodents like guinea pigs, hamsters, gerbils, rats and mi**
- **fishes and frogs**
- **dogs and monkeys**

I made a slide that looked at the good and bad things about animal testing. I think I should have put more pictures on this slide because it looks boring.

Is animal testing good or bad?

BAD!
- Some people think it is **bad**. They think animal testing is cruel and inhuman. It is morally wrong to torture animals for our own benefit. Over 3 million animals have been tormented all in the name of research.
- But this is an opinion, not a fact. I think that it is a good opinion but some people don't.

GOOD!
The other argument is that thousands of people are saved from painful diseases and death by powerful medical drugs and treatments. This incredible gift of medicine would not be possible without animal testing.
This person thinks it is good. The website is an English teaching site. I think that it is an opinion, because it says this on the site, and I don't think it is a reliable website.

Teacher says:
This student has clearly focused her presentation on a younger audience, and explains this well in her annotation. Images are used appropriately. The student could have used fewer colours and still made the site colourful and interesting.

The images are not too horrid, because children would be upset by them.

Teacher says: *Annotation is good, as it explains why the student put certain things into her presentation. She identifies some ways in which she could improve the presentation.*

Model answer Level 6

To achieve a Level 6 you will need to:

✓ Base searches on clear criteria, using advanced searches to get more relevant results

✓ Check validity of sources and select appropriate information

✓ Design and format a presentation to be appropriate for your audience, including rewriting text and selecting appropriate images

✓ Evaluate your presentation by checking it against a given brief, and revise work accordingly

✓ Explain your working processes clearly in your annotation

I searched on 'animal testing' using Google Advanced Search. This meant that I got back more up-to-date results.

I also tried using OR and NOT searches to see if the results were any better.

Slide 3 – Title: Arguments for Animal Testing

Antibiotics, HIV drugs, insulin and cancer drugs rely on animal tests because other testing methods aren't advanced enough.

URL - http://www.bbc.co.uk/science/hottopics/animalexperiments/index.shtml

This information is factual. The information may not be valid anymore because the date of the information is 2004, so there may be more up-to-date information available. I found a report from 2006 that said there were other ways of testing these drugs now. (http://www.medicalnewstoday.com/medicalnews.php?newsid=39985).
The information is not biased, because the website it was found on also tried to put the other point of view as well.

Animal experiments are only allowed when there is no alternative, and when there are more advantages than disadvantages.

I found several websites that gave different views on animal testing. I rewrote the information I found so it was easy to understand for Year 7 pupils.

Teacher says: *This student has completed a very thorough research sheet, which shows his sources and comments on validity and bias.*
This will be a very useful tool for the student to use when designing the actual presentation.

Teacher says: *The student has used a variety of sources to get information. He also explains in his annotation how he rewrote the text to be appropriate to his audience of Year 7 students.*

I copied the text from my research sheet into my presentation. This slide shows the arguments for animal testing. I included one for and one against, so I wasn't biased.

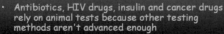

Arguments for animal testing
☑
- Antibiotics, HIV drugs, insulin and cancer drugs rely on animal tests because other testing methods aren't advanced enough
  - http://www.bbc.co.uk/science/hottopics/animalexperiments/index.shtml
- Animal experiments are only allowed when there is no alternative, and when there are more benefits than disadvantages
  - http://www.homeoffice.gov.uk/science-research/animal-testing/
- Strict laws ensure animals are kept in good conditions, and are killed in a humane way so they don't suffer
  - http://www.homeoffice.gov.uk/science-research/animal-testing/

This picture is meant to show that this slide is about the arguments for animal testing.

If I had more time, I would improve my presentation by including more images, because children would like more pictures.

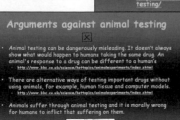

Arguments against animal testing
☒
- Animal testing can be dangerously misleading. It doesn't always show what would happen to humans taking the same drug. An animal's response to a drug can be different to a human's
  - http://www.bbc.co.uk/science/hottopics/animalexperiments/index.shtml
- There are alternative ways of testing important drugs without using animals, for example, human tissue and computer models.
  - http://www.bbc.co.uk/science/hottopics/animalexperiments/index.shtml
- Animals suffer through animal testing and it is morally wrong for humans to inflict that suffering on them.

Teacher says: *The student has created an effective presentation that doesn't go overboard on colour, but looks good. The colours and fonts look like they will appeal to teenagers. He has also suggested some improvements that he could make to make it even more appropriate for his intended audience.*

UNIT

Unit introduction

In this unit you are going to be the manager of a new teen band called The Shakes. You've got big plans for them – they are great musicians and have some really catchy songs. They also put on a great live performance and already have a growing fan base.

However, they aren't very good with money! They've brought you in to help them sort out the business side of the band, to make sure they don't end up in the bargain bucket too early on in their career!

You are going to be creating a business model for the band, in order to keep track of how much money they are spending and how much they are making.

Unit learning objectives

We are learning to:

- Develop models by adding or changing variables and rules
- Create charts based on data in the model
- Develop interrogation skills including the use of **Goal Seek**
- Explore a model and draw conclusions
- Prepare a presentation showing and explaining information to a given audience

Unit preparation

1. You will need to set up a folder in your area and name it **Unit 8.4 – Band Manager**.

2. You will need to know how to enter text, data and formulae into a spreadsheet, and format cells.

3. You should be able to create simple charts using the **Chart Wizard**.

Start thinking about ...

Models

A **model** is a replica (copy) of a system that enables us to investigate what happens to the system when certain things change.

A model can show you what might happen in different scenarios – for example, how many people would have to buy a CD in order to cover the cost of recording it, or what price it would need to be to make a certain amount of profit.

A spreadsheet is a piece of software that allows us to create a model of a system, like a company's finances.

Step 1.1

Shake 'em up!

The Shakes have recently launched their first single 'Shake 'em up'. They have printed 2,000 copies of the single, and want to know if they are going to make a profit on it.

Look at the model on **CD Resource 1c – Shake 'em up spreadsheet**, which shows you how much money they have had to pay out to produce the single (**Costs**), and how much money they have made so far on single sales (**Revenue**).

Complete Activity 1 on the spreadsheet.

£1000

Step 1.2

Find an outcome using Goal Seek

We can make answering the type of queries you made in questions 9–11 a lot easier by using a tool called **Goal Seek**. This allows us to tell the spreadsheet what we want an output to be, such as £1,000 profit, and what cell we want it to alter to reach this figure.

Step 1.3

Select the output

Click in the cell that you want to show your **output**. For example, if you want to find out how many CDs would need to be sold to make £1,000 profit, the output is the profit, so you need to click in the cell that shows Profit/Loss. On your spreadsheet, this is cell **E20**.

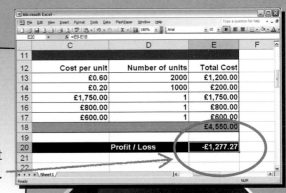

Step 1.4

Set values in Goal Seek

With cell **E20** selected, choose **Tools > Goal Seek**.

In the **To value** box, type in the output value you want to see. In this case, it is **1000**, because you want to see how many CDs you need to sell to make £1,000 profit.

In the **By changing cell** box, type in the input cell reference (that's the cell you want the spreadsheet to calculate a new value for). In this case, it is **D7** – the cell that shows CD sales.

Click **OK**. Goal Seek will change the value in cell **D7** to show how many CDs the band needs to sell to make £1000 profit.

Now try to answer the remaining questions on the spreadsheet using Goal Seek (Activity 2).

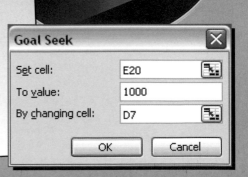

UNIT

Tutorial 2 Creating and interrogating a model

The band are anxious that they are not selling enough CDs. They have decided to do a tour to promote the single, and make more sales. They are going to give you some figures and they want you to calculate if they will make a profit or a loss from the tour.

By the end of this tutorial you will be able to:

- Extract information and reorganise it in a more useful form
- Construct formulae to calculate revenue, costs and profit
- Perform calculations using **Goal Seek**

Step 2.1

Reorganise information into a more useful form

Open **CD Resource 2c – Tour figures** and read the email from the band, which contains some financial information about their tour. The information is not very clear, though.

First, enter the figures in the email into the table below it. You should find figures for **Price per unit**, **Unit sales**, **Cost per unit** and **Units bought**.

Revenue	Price per unit	Unit sales
Ticket sales		
Single sales		
T-shirts		

Costs	Cost per unit	Units bought
Venue hire		
Travel, hotel and food		
Advertising		
T-shirts		

Step 2.2

Construct a basic model

Open **CD Resource 2d – Tour spreadsheet**. You can now copy and paste the figures from your table into the correct cells in the spreadsheet. Select the figures you want to copy, then choose **Edit > Copy** (or right-click on the selected figures and choose **Copy**).

Then go to the spreadsheet and select the cells you want to paste the figures into, and choose **Edit > Paste**.

	A	B	C	D	E
1		The Shakes tour spreadsheet			
2			Price per unit	Unit sales	Total
3		Revenue			
4		Ticket sales			
5		Single sales			
6		T-shirts			
7		Total revenue			
8					
9			Cost per unit	Units bought	Total
10		Costs			
11		Venue hire			
12		Travel costs			
13		Advertising			
14		T-shirts			
15		Total costs			
16					
17				Profit/Loss	
18					

Step 2.3

Creating formulae

The next step is to enter formulae in **Column E** on the spreadsheet. You need to enter formulae to calculate revenue and costs for each product line, Total revenue, Total costs and Profit/Loss.

Points to remember:

- Your formulae must always begin with =
- Use cell references in your formulae so that you can copy formulae for product lines from one cell into the next.

=C5*D5

+ means add
(You can also use SUM, for example: =SUM(B6:H6) will add numbers in cells from B6 to H6)

- means subtract
* means multiply
/ means divide

Step 2.4

Enter formulae into a model

Enter a formula for ticket sales in cell **E4** on the spreadsheet. Remember that you can click in the cells you want to use rather than typing the cell reference in.

Then click on the **Fill Handle** and drag the formula into the next two product lines (**cells E5:E6**).

Do the same thing for the Costs section of the table, dragging the formula into cells **E12:E14**.

Step 2.5

Using AutoSum ∑

The **AutoSum ∑** tool can be used to add lists of numbers together very quickly.

The easiest way to do this is to first select the range of cells you want to add. Then simply click on the **AutoSum ∑** symbol on the **Standard toolbar**. The formula for the sum will then be added to the cell directly below the list of numbers you have added.

Step 2.6

Use Goal Seek to calculate input values

As you learned in Tutorial 1, you can choose an **output** value and use **Goal Seek** to calculate the required **input** value.

Examples of output values on your model are Total revenue and Profit/Loss.

Examples of input values are ticket price and number of tickets sold.

Using Goal Seek, we can find out the price we need to charge, or the number we need to sell to make a set level of profit.

Band Manager

Tutorial 3 Using absolute cell referencing

The tour was a great success, and single sales have taken off! The band are very happy with your model, but now they've made so much money the tax man is chasing them for VAT (Value Added Tax). You are going to help them work out their VAT so they don't all end up behind bars!

By the end of this tutorial you will be able to:
- Add additional columns and new variables to a spreadsheet model
- Use an absolute cell reference to calculate VAT

Step 3.1

Different kinds of cell referencing

There are two types of cell referencing: **relative cell referencing** and **absolute cell referencing**. Absolute cell references contain dollar signs ($) as shown on the right.

> Relative cell referencing:
> $$=C4*D4$$
>
> Absolute cell referencing:
> $$=\$C\$4*D4$$

Step 3.2

Relative cell referencing

If you want cell references to change when you copy a formula, use **relative cell referencing**. In your Tour spreadsheet model, you used relative cell referencing so that you could drag the formula into the boxes below, and it would automatically change the cell references.

To write a relative cell reference, you just need to write the cell references.

	C	D	
2	Price per unit	Unit sales	Total
3			
4	12	300	=C4*D4
5	2	200	=C5*D5
6	15	150	=C6*D6
7			

Step 3.3

Absolute cell referencing

You use **absolute cell referencing** when you want all the formulae in a series to refer to one cell. For example, if you want to apply a 10% discount to all your prices, you can type the discount into one cell, and then make all your formulae refer back to that cell.

To write an absolute cell reference, you should add dollar signs ($) in front of the letter and number in the cell reference of the cell you always want to refer to, as shown in the example on the right.

Tip: The quickest way to make a cell reference absolute is to click in the cell reference and press F4 on your keyboard.

	A	B	C	D	E	F
1		The Shakes tour spreadsheet				
2			Price per unit	Unit sales		Discount
3		Revenue				
4		Ticket sales	12	300		=C4*C9
5		Single sales	2	200		
6		T-shirts	15	150		
7		Total revenue				
8						
9		Discount %	10%			
10						

In the example above, you can see it is the green cell reference that is absolute, because it contains the $ signs. This will stay the same when the formula is copied into the cells below.

The blue cell reference will change when it is copied, because it is a relative cell reference.

Tutorial 3 | Using absolute cell referencing

Step 3.4

Add new columns to an existing model

To add VAT to your Tour spreadsheet, you need to add new columns.

To do this, first select the column **to the right** of where you want your new column to go. Then choose **Insert > Columns**. The new column will appear to the left of the column you selected. You can then add headings at the top of the new columns. Find and open **CD Resource 3d – Screenshot showing added columns** to see where you need to put new columns, and what you need to name them.

Step 3.5

Add the VAT rate to your spreadsheet

You are going to use absolute cell referencing to calculate the VAT that needs to be added to everything the band sells, so you need to add the VAT rate to a cell. That cell is your absolute cell reference. Put it in cell **C17**.

You can now type in a formula to calculate the VAT on ticket price in cell **D4**.

Remember, the formula must always refer back to cell **C17**.

Step 3.6

Copy a formula into other cells in a series

Once you have entered your formula for working out VAT, you can drag it into the cells directly below to show the VAT that will be added to **Singles** and **T-shirts**.

Step 3.7

Calculate price including VAT

Calculating the price including VAT is easy – you just need to add the price *excluding* VAT to the VAT! Do you need to use a relative or an absolute cell reference for this formula?

You should find it relatively easy now to complete the spreadsheet model. Complete the **Costs** section in the same way as the **Revenue** section.

8.4 Band Manager

Yourbands
Free Music Downloads **MP3**
Start Here

UNIT

Tutorial 4 Creating and using charts

The band are keen to see what effect their tour has had on the sales of their single. It has been available to download on a website for several weeks, but it hasn't been doing too well up to now. They want you to analyse the data on the website and produce a chart so that they can see if the single is selling better now.

By the end of this tutorial you will be able to:

- Copy and paste data into a spreadsheet and sort it usefully
- Create a chart and add a new series

Step 4.1

Select and copy data in a table

You can copy and paste tables from word-processing documents or web pages into a spreadsheet.

Open **CD Resource 4a – Yourbands download chart**.

Select the table by hovering your mouse over the top left-hand corner until the square with the arrows appears on the corner. Click on this to select the whole table, then choose **Edit > Copy**.

Yourbands Download Chart	
Band name	**Single name**
The Bone Scrapers	Serious Fun
The Fabuloso Sisters	Scream if you wanna go faster
Metalmonkey	Chained Melody
The Shakes	Shake 'em Up
Blistercreep	Headcase
Shark Girls	Pretty in Purple
The Creeps	I'm in love (with myself)
Rumblefish	How cool is she?
Moonjuicer	Rocket Science
M and M	Baby give it back

Step 4.2

Paste data into a spreadsheet

Open a new spreadsheet document. Click in a cell near the top left-hand corner, for example, cell **B2** and choose **Edit > Paste**. The data will then be placed in the spreadsheet.

You may need to adjust row heights and column widths. To do this, click and drag on the row and column dividers on the grey edges of the sheet.

Step 4.3

Sort data in a spreadsheet

The Yourbands download chart is not in any order. This makes it hard to read. It would be easier to see how the band's single is selling in comparison to the other bands if the data was **sorted**.

You can sort the data by different columns. You are going to sort by **Column D – No. of downloads last week**.

Click in a cell in the table in **Column D**, then choose **Data > Sort**. In the **Sort by** box, make sure **No. of downloads last week** is showing.

Then click the radio button that reads **Descending**, and click **OK**. The table will now be sorted to show highest number of downloads first.

SMART SKILLS BUILDER **ICT** YR8

Tutorial 4 — Creating and using charts

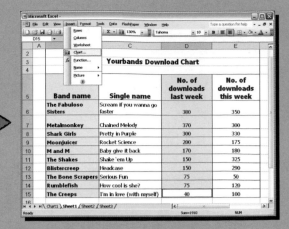

Step 4.4

Create a bar chart

You are now going to make a **bar chart** to show how the single was selling last week. Select the data in **Columns B** and **D** (keep **Ctrl** pressed down to select two columns). Then choose **Insert > Chart**.

In Microsoft Excel, bar charts are called 'Column charts'. Select one, then click through to **Step 4**. Click the radio button to place your chart on a new sheet. Click **Finish**.

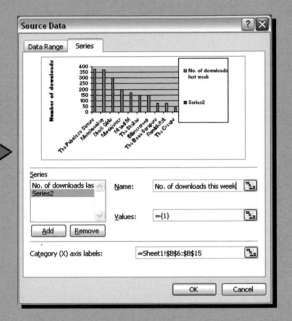

Step 4.5

Add a second series to a chart

To see how the single is doing this week compared to last week, you can add this data series to your chart. Right-click anywhere in the chart area and choose **Source Data**.

There are two tabs in the box that opens. Go to the second tab (labelled **Series**). Below the Series window on the left, click **Add**.

You will see a new series appear, called **Series2**. In the **Name** box on the right, type in **No. of downloads this week**.

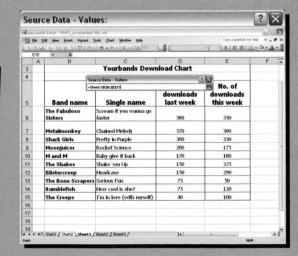

Step 4.6

Select a data range for the new series

In the **Values** box, you need to select the column in your table for **No. of downloads this week**. Click on the little red, white and blue square on the right of the text box.

This will take you back to your chart. Go to the worksheet containing your table, and select the column for **No. of downloads this week**, as shown on the right. In the long, thin **Source Data** box, click on the symbol with the red arrow. Click **OK**.

The new series will be placed in your chart, next to the first series.

What can you see about how The Shakes' single is selling this week compared to last week?

Band Manager

Tutorial 5 Extending and formatting a model

The Shakes are doing really well now, and they have attracted interest from a major record label. They have asked you to make some revisions to the model you created for them, and to make it look really good for the record company.

By the end of this tutorial you will be able to:

- Add variables to a model and consider the outcome of these changes
- Revise values in a spreadsheet and save a new version
- Format the model to be clearly readable and suitable to present to a company

Step 5.1

Change variables in a spreadsheet model

The model on the right shows the band's finances before their tour – this is now out-of-date. You need to enter new variables for single sales, now that the band are doing so well. Open **CD Resource 5b – Revenue and costs (old)**, and enter the following variables in the **Revenue** section:

- Unit sales (CD) – 1856
- Unit sales (Downloads) – 2050

Step 5.2

Add new rows to a spreadsheet model

You also need to insert two new rows in the model, to add the revenue and costs of the tour. Right-click on the grey number at the end of the row and choose **Insert** from the popup menu. The new row will appear *above* the row you selected.

Insert two new rows in the **Revenue** section, and two new rows in the **Costs** section of your model.

Step 5.3

Add new variables to a spreadsheet model

Open **CD Resource 5a – Final tour figures** and follow the instructions on the sheet to copy and paste the information from the table into the **Revenue** and **Costs** sections of your model.

Your model should now look something like the one shown on the right. Expand **Column B** to fit the new text in the **Costs** section.

Step 5.4

Revise formulae to take account of new variables

You now need to change the formulae to take your new variables into account.

Click and drag on the **Revenue** and **Costs** formulae to copy them into the new cells. Then double-click in the cells showing the formulae for **Total revenue** and **Total costs**, and revise the formulae to include the new cells. You can do this by pulling down the handle on the blue box containing the original series (**E7:E8**) to include cells **E9** and **E10**.

es	Total Revenue
1856	£5,549.44
2050	£1,640.00
	£3,540.00
	£1,440.00
	=SUM(E6:E7)

Step 5.5

Format fonts and align text

You are going to present your spreadsheet to a record company, so it must be easy to read, and look good.

First make sure you have used the same font and font size throughout, and that all important titles and figures are in bold.

Centering text and numbers is a good way of making columns easier to read. Usually, text aligns to the left, and numbers align to the right, so column headings can be out of line. To centre data, select all the cells you want to align and click on the **Centre Align** symbol ≣ on the formatting toolbar.

Step 5.6

Add borders to a spreadsheet

Borders are important for making a spreadsheet easy to read. To make a border, first select the cells you want to apply the border to. Then click on the arrow next to the **Borders** symbol on the formatting toolbar. You can then choose the border you want.

Select **All Borders** to create a grid. Select **No Border** to clear all borders – useful if you make a mistake! A thick box border can be used to frame the whole table.

Step 5.7

Add colour to a spreadsheet

Finally, you can add colour to highlight particular rows, columns or cells. Try not to use too many colours; or your model will become more difficult to read.

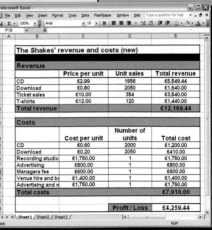

UNIT

Tutorial 6 Presenting work

In this tutorial you are going to prepare to present your spreadsheet model to a major record company. The company are impressed with the band, but you have to show them that the band really are doing the business in financial terms!

By the end of this tutorial you will be able to:

- Display a spreadsheet showing formulae
- Add a spreadsheet table and chart to a presentation document
- Annotate your work to explain your working processes

Step 6.1

Set up a presentation document

Open a new presentation document and save it to your folder. Create five new slides and give them suitable titles.

You are going to include the following three documents in your presentation:

CD Resource 6a – Revenue and costs (old)
Revenue and costs (new) (your own saved version)
Yourbands download chart (your own saved version)

The first page should be the title page, and the last page should include a written evaluation of your work.

Step 6.2

Add a spreadsheet table to a presentation document

You can add a spreadsheet table to a presentation as a spreadsheet object. To do this, select all the cells in your table. Then choose **Edit > Copy**. Go to the page in your presentation where you want to paste the table, and choose **Edit > Paste Special**. Select **Microsoft Office Excel Worksheet object** and click **OK**. Then double-click on the table.

Tip: Do not try to paste the table into a text box – this will cause chaos in your data!

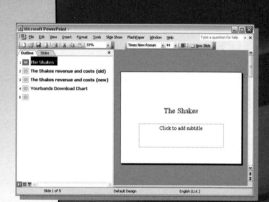

Step 6.3

Edit a spreadsheet table within a presentation document

You can edit the spreadsheet object as necessary. For example, you may find the font size is too small to read very well, so needs to be enlarged.

To edit any formatting elements in the table, double-click on the table, right-click on it and choose **Format Cells**.

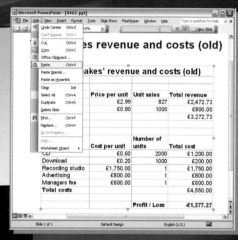

Step 6.4

Insert a spreadsheet chart into a presentation

To copy and paste a chart into a presentation, click in the white area around the chart, and choose **Edit > Copy**. (Note: You cannot use right-click and copy for this action.)

Go to the page in your presentation where you want to paste the table, and choose **Edit > Paste Special**. Carry on as **Step 6.2**.

You can then double-click on the chart to format it.

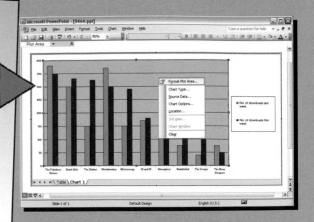

Step 6.5

View formulae in a spreadsheet

Sometimes it is useful to be able to show the formulae in a table, rather than showing the values. This makes it easy to check that the formulae are correct.

To do this, make sure you are still in Excel and choose **Tools > Options**. In the window that appears, select the **View** tab. In **Windows options**, click in the **Formulas** box, then click **OK**.

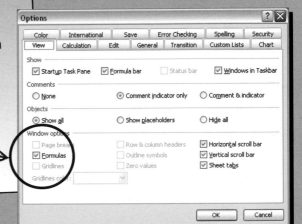

Step 6.6

Add the table to your presentation

Now your spreadsheet will show the formulae. Add another page in your presentation and insert the table showing the formulae on to this page (see **Step 6.2**).

You will need to adjust column widths to resize your table to an appropriate size.

Costs			
	Cost per unit	Number of units	Total cost
CD	0.6	2000	=C14*D14
Download	0.2	=D7	=C15*D15
Recording studio	1750	1	=C16*D16
Advertising	800	1	=C17*D17
Managers fee	600	1	=C18*D18
Venue hire and ban	1400	1	=C19*D19
Advertising and me	1750	1	=C20*D20
Total costs			=SUM(E14:E20)
		Profit / Loss	=E10-E21

Step 6.7

Annotate your presentation

Once you have added your tables and chart to the presentation, you need to annotate it to explain what each slide is showing. You can do this either using the **Add Notes** section at the bottom of each slide, or by using text boxes.

On your final slide, write an evaluation of your work through this unit.

Tip: Think about what the record company bosses might be specifically interested in.

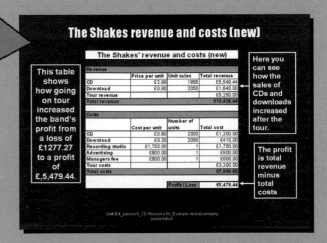

Unit assessment
Reckless Records Ltd

Introduction

The Shakes have now been given a record deal. Their record company, Reckless Records Ltd, want to run a major marketing campaign to launch the band's first album. Part of this campaign will be a band website, calendar, posters, and even a TV advert!

You will have to produce a spreadsheet model to show the record company whether all these things are possible in order for them to make a profit.

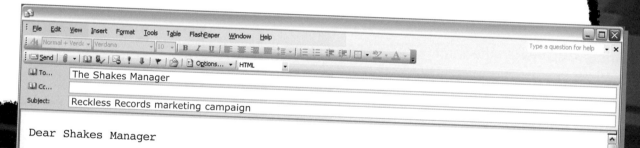

File Edit View Insert Format Tools Table FlashPaper Window Help

Normal + Verda ▾ | Verdana ▾ | 10 ▾ | B I U | ▤ ▤ ▤ ▤ | ▤ ▾ | ▤ ▤ ▤ ▤ | ▢ ▾ ▭ ▾ A ▾

Type a question for help ▾ ✕

Send | ⬚ ▾ | ⬚ ⬚ | ⬚ ▾ | ⬚ ! ⬚ ▾ | ⬚ | ⬚ Options... ▾ | HTML ▾

To...   The Shakes Manager
Cc...
Subject: Reckless Records marketing campaign

Dear Shakes Manager

We are writing to you regarding the marketing campaign for The Shakes' new album, 'Shaker Rebellion'. We have several ideas for promoting the album, including a website, a range of new merchandise and a TV advertising campaign.

We have started to produce a spreadsheet that shows the revenue and costs of each activity, and we would like you to complete the spreadsheet to see if we are going to make a profit.

We are a bit worried about the cost of the TV advertising campaign. We have worked out that a radio advertising campaign could generate the same album sales, and will be exactly half the cost. Please can you also produce a version of the spreadsheet that shows the model with the cost of the radio advertising campaign instead of the TV campaign?

We need to generate at least £20,000 profit from this campaign. In both spreadsheets, can you work out the minimum number of albums we need to sell, assuming that everything else remains the same?

We look forward to seeing your two spreadsheets.

Kind regards,
Rob Reckless
Marketing Director
Reckless Records Ltd

Unit assessment: Reckless Records Ltd

Assessment tips:

- Open **CD Resource 8b** and save it as **Unit 8.4 Unit assessment** in your folder **Unit 8.4 – Band Manager**.

- Complete the tasks on the spreadsheet in order. If you miss a step, your results may not be correct and all your other answers may be wrong.

- Once you have completed the first table, copy and paste it into the second worksheet in the spreadsheet document. Then you can revise it to show the radio advertising campaign costs.

- Format your tables so that they are clear to read by someone who is not an expert on spreadsheets!

Glossary of key words

Absolute cell reference	A cell reference that remains the same when copied to other cells. Dollar signs '$' are used to keep a column and/or row reference constant. For example, **B6** will always refer to cell **B6**.	**Input value**	Information or data that is entered into a computer to alter a model.
AutoSum	This feature, shown by the Sigma symbol '$\sum$' automatically adds up the value of a sequence of selected cells.	**Model**	A mathematical replica (copy) of a system that enables us to investigate what happens to the system when certain things change. A spreadsheet is an example of a piece of software that allows us to build a model.
Chart series	Each set of separate data displayed on a chart. For example, temperatures in the UK/temperatures in Spain.	**Output value**	Information that comes from a computer after it has been processed by the computer.
Goal Seek	This tool attempts to obtain the optimum input to reach a given output value. This can also be called **what-if analysis**.	**Relative cell reference**	A basic type of cell reference that changes when it is copied into other cells. It is the most commonly used cell reference for formulae.

UNIT

Model answer Level 5

To achieve a Level 5 you will need to:

✓ Explore the effects of changing the variables in an ICT-based model

✓ Use Goal Seek to identify the required input value to gain a set output

✓ Create an appropriate chart comparing two data series

✓ Create an annotated report for a given audience

In this table I put the new revenue and costs into the old spreadsheet to see if the profit would change. The profit has gone up. I copied the formulae into the new cells.

Here are the new figures for CDs and Downloads. I had to add another row for Tour revenue. This makes the profit go up.

Revenue and costs (new)

Revenue	Price per unit	Unit sales	Total
CD	2.99	1856	£5,549.44
Download	0.8	2050	£1,640.00
Tour revenue			£6,250.00
Total revenue			£13,439.44
Costs			
			Total cost
CD	0.6	2000	£1,200.00
Download	0.2	2050	£410.00
Recording studio	1750	1	£1,750.00
Advertising	800	1	£800.00
Managers fee	600	1	£600.00
Tour costs			£3,200.00
Total costs			£7,960.00
		Profit/Loss	£5,479.44

The band have to make a profit so this is good. You can see that they are making £5479.44 in profit.

I wanted to make the presentation look good for the record company so I formatted some of the cells in different colours and fonts.

Teacher says: *This student has created a working model, and changed variables to see the effects on the model. She has referred to her audience in her annotation, and explained what she has done to address them. Her annotation could have explained what the model is showing in greater detail, and drawn some conclusions about why this is important for the band and the record company.*

I made a bar chart of the download data from the Yourbands website. This shows sales for this week and last week.

The chart is good because you can see who is doing the best.

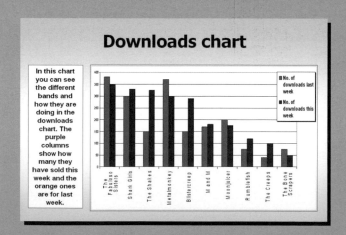

Downloads chart

In this chart you can see the different bands and how they are doing in the downloads chart. The purple columns show how many they have sold this week and the orange ones are for last week.

- No. of downloads last week
- No. of downloads this week

Teacher says: *The student has been able to create a chart showing two series, but does not explain why this is useful (to compare the band's popularity before and after their tour). The student has annotated the chart, but only to describe what it shows – this is not necessary as the chart shows this well enough anyway. The annotation should focus on the conclusions that can be drawn from the data if the student is to achieve a higher level.*

Model answer Level 6

To achieve a Level 6 you will need to:

✓ Meet all the success criteria for Level 5

✓ Use spreadsheet models to make predictions and vary rules within the models

✓ Annotate your work, drawing conclusions from your findings

✓ Check how well your model works, and suggest improvements

I changed variables in the spreadsheet to show how the tour affected the single sales. I also used Goal Seek to see how many singles the band needed to sell to make different profit levels.

My presentation was for a record company so it needed to look professional. I used the same background and fonts on all slides.

It is hard to compare the old and new spreadsheets, because they are on separate slides. I could make a chart to show the old and new profit levels.

The Shakes revenue and costs

This table shows how going on tour increased the band's profit from a loss of £1277.27 to a profit of £5,479.44.

The Shakes' revenue and costs (new)

Revenue

	Price per unit	Unit sales	Total revenue
CD	£2.99	1856	£5,549.44
Download	£0.80	2050	£1,640.00
Tour revenue			£6,250.00
Total revenue			£13,439.44

Costs

	Cost per unit	Number of units	Total cost
CD	£0.60	2000	£1,200.00
Download	£0.20	2050	£410.00
Recording studio	£1,750.00	1	£1,750.00
Advertising	£800.00	1	£800.00
Managers fee	£600.00	1	£600.00
Tour costs			£3,200.00
Total costs			£7,960.00
		Profit / Los	£5,479.44

Unit sales of CDs and downloads have both more than doubled.

The profit has risen by £6756.71 compared to before the tour

Teacher says: *This student has created a good working model and explored it using spreadsheet tools such as Goal Seek. He has changed variables in the model to see what would happen to profit. His report is well designed and is appropriate to show to the target audience – the record company management. The student also draws conclusions from the model, and attempts to explain these for the audience.*

I made a chart to show the single sales last week. I then added a new series to my chart to compare the sales for this week.

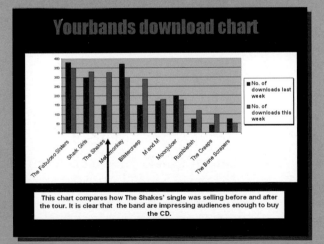

Yourbands download chart

This chart compares how The Shakes' single was selling before and after the tour. It is clear that the band are impressing audiences enough to buy the CD.

It is good to add the second series to the chart because you can show the record company how the single sales have improved without going to another spreadsheet.

Teacher says: *The student has shown he is able to add a series to a chart and his annotation shows that he understands the value of doing this. The annotation is detailed and shows that the student had a good understanding of the purpose of the tasks he completed, drawn conclusions from it, and has thought about how he might improve his work.*

UNIT

Unit introduction

This unit is all about the process of designing a computer game for a specific audience – children aged between 5 and 9 years of age. The theme of the game is to teach children about the importance of eating five portions of fruit and vegetables a day.

Working in a small team you will research classic and modern computer games, create and use questionnaires, and design all the game elements. Finally, you will be required to put together a game design proposal for a computer games company – GamePlan IT.

Unit learning objectives

We are learning to:

- Work as part of a team
- Use digital-based research techniques
- Create and use questionnaires in Microsoft Excel
- Design game elements using Scratch software
- Write a game design proposal

GamePlan IT seek experienced game designers for new educational project

Ever wanted to have a go at designing educational computer games? Well now is your chance. GamePlan IT seek tenders to develop a Scratch game for children aged between 5 and 9

The game must -
- be fun to play
- teach children about the 5-a-day healthy eating [...]
- incorporate different levels and degrees of diffi[...]
- be optimised for delivery over the Internet

Apply in writing to:

Unit preparation

1. You will need to set up a folder in your area and name it **Unit 8.5 – GamePlan IT**.
2. You will need to have a basic understanding of the **Scratch** software package.

Start thinking about ...

Computer game classification

When computer games are being planned, it is important that the designers ensure they are age-appropriate.

Computer games, like films, need an age-range classification if the game contains sexual, violent or drug-related content. The **British Board of Film Classification** (BBFC) is responsible for classifying video games.

Some people worry about the effect some games may have on children and feel that all computer games should have an age classification.

Do you agree with this or do you think it is all a fuss about nothing?

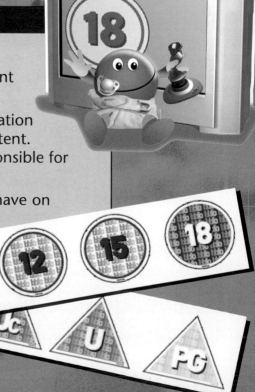

Step 1.1

Research different game designs

Over the last few years some hugely successful games for children have been produced, such as Sonic the Hedgehog, Breakout and Tetris.

Using a search engine such as Google, find and play a range of classic and modern arcade-style games and make notes about their features, using **CD Resource 1a – Computer game research**.

What is good about each game? Why do you think the games are so successful?

For each game think about graphics, music and audio, game function, game play difficulty, extra levels, hidden/secret rewards, etc.

Step 1.2

Annotate your work

In Scratch, you can add comments in the **Scripts area** to annotate your work. You can also right-click on the **Stage** and the **Scripts area** and **save picture of scripts**.

Throughout this unit, you will need to use annotation to show your working processes, for example, to explain:

- Different ideas you have about game play
- How you solved technical aspects such as game functionality
- The scripts that make things happen in the game

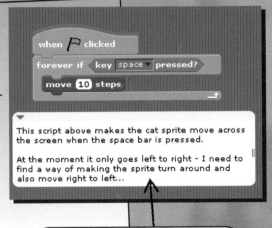

Add comments within the Scripts area to annotate your work

Step 1.3

Make and add screenshots

Press the **Print Screen** key at any time to capture a copy of the whole computer screen to the clipboard. You can then **Paste** this image into a suitable program (for example, a word-processing program) and annotate the image.

Screenshots can be used for many different purposes in computer game design. They can be used to show another programmer what you have done, or to show the users (people playing the game) how to play the game better.

GamePlan IT

Tutorial 2 Game questionnaire

In this tutorial, you will focus on how to use an Excel spreadsheet to create a questionnaire to find out what sort of computer games your friends use. You will use data validation techniques to make sure the information you get is appropriate.

By the end of this tutorial you will be able to use Excel to:

- Create an interactive questionnaire
- Distribute your questionnaire and analyse results
- Validate the data you collect to make sure it is correct

Step 2.1

Write questions

Before a company designs a new game, they have to do some **market research** to find out what games people are playing, and what they want in a new game.

Write 8–10 questions to ask your friends about computer games. Plan your questions carefully – they need to inform you of a users' interest in games and what they are looking for in a new game.

Computer games questionnaire

1. How often in the week do you play games?

2. Are you male or female?

3. What is the average time you play a game?

4. What type of game do you like?
   Rate each type 0–10 (0 = don't like 10 = love it!)

5. Do you prefer learning through games?

6. What are some features of games that you like?

Step 2.2

Set up a questionnaire in Excel

Open a new spreadsheet and type your questions as shown on the right.

Enter each question in the first column (**column A**). Drag on the column header to widen the row to fit your longest question.

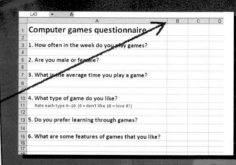

Step 2.3

Types of question

For each question, decide on the type of answer you expect to see, for example: **Yes/No**, a **number** or a **comment**.

Most questions can be created with dropdown response menus in a spreadsheet. This makes it harder for someone to type in a wrong response. We call this kind of control **data validation**.

To add a dropdown box, select the cell where you want the answer to appear. Then on the top menu select **Data > Validation**. Select **List** in the **Allow** dropdown list and in **Source** type your responses, separated by commas. Click **OK**.

A dropdown box should now appear with your responses.

Step 2.4

Other types of data

Using the same technique, now add dropdown boxes for other answer types, for example, to show male or female, or number of hours games are played.

Are you male or female?

Male
Female

Step 2.5

Plot a chart to show a response

To look at interest in different types of games you can use a **rating response** (an example is shown on the right) and create a chart from this.

Highlight the titles and the numbers in your table. Select **Insert > Chart** and find the **Column chart**. Click **Next** until the final screen in the Wizard, then click **Finish**.

When the chart appears, position it on your questionnaire. The chart will automatically plot as the ratings are filled in.

What type of game do you like?	Strategy	Action	Shooter	Sports	Arcade	Puzzle
Rate each type 0-10 (0=don't like 10=love it!)	3	5	8	5	9	1

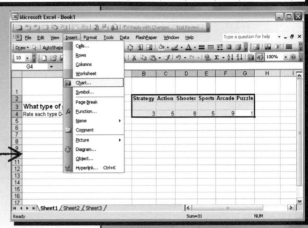

Strategy	Action	Shooter	Sports	Arcade	Puzzle
3	5	8	5	9	1

Step 2.6

Further use of data validation

You can also control the numbers people type into boxes. This will stop anyone putting in 'dirty' data (such as letters or high numbers that will stop the chart working properly).

Highlight the cells where the numbers will be entered. Choose **Data > Validation**.

Choose **Whole number** in the Allow box and choose **between** in the Data box. Then type in Minimum **0 (zero)** and Maximum **10**. Click **OK**.

This will stop people typing in letters or numbers higher than 10. Try typing 200 into one of the cells and see what happens. You should get an error message.

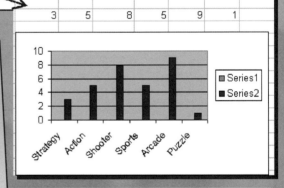

Step 2.7

Present your questionnaire

You could improve the look of your questionnaire by using colour fills and outlines if you have time.

What type of game do you like?	Strategy	Action	Shoot
Rate each type 0-10 (0=don't like 10=love it!)			

UNIT

Tutorial 3 Handling movement

Movement of characters and other objects is a fundamental part of modern computer games. Generally a user can control the movement of their own character (sometimes called an **avatar**) through a virtual landscape.

The avatar may be required to run, jump or roll. Objects may float, fall or bounce. All these types of movement need to be programmed into the game.

By the end of this tutorial you will be able to:

- Learn different ways of controlling movement in Scratch
- Apply coding techniques to create movement in games

Step 3.1

Continuous movement

Open **CD Resource 3d – Continuous movement**. This sample script shows a simple way of enabling sprite movement using the **colour is touching** script block (from the **Sensing menu**).

Click on the **Green Flag** to play the script. In this example, the sprite moves continually in one direction (in Scratch, this is referred to as **forever**) while the red dot is touching the white part of the background.

Try changing the script. Can you make the sprite move when it is on the blue background and stop when it touches the white?

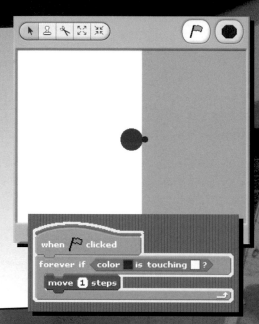

Step 3.2

User-controlled movement

In most computer games, the user needs to have more control over movement.

Open **CD Resource 3d – User-controlled movement**. You can control the sprite's movement by using the left and right arrows on your keyboard. The script also changes the sprite's **orientation** (which way it is facing) using the **point in direction** script block.

Can you add two new scripts to make the sprite move up and down, using the up and down arrows?

Step 3.3

Challenge activity!

Try to edit the script that controls movement to the left so that the sprite will only move when it is on the **white** background.

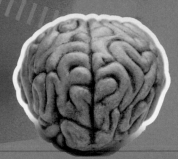

Tutorial 3 Handling movement

Step 3.4

Jump to it!

Open **CD Resource 3d – Jump movement**. Click the **Green Flag** to start the script. Press the space bar to make the blue sprite jump over the moving sprite.

This script changes the **vertical (y)** position of the blue sprite – firstly upwards, using a positive (+) number and then downwards, using a negative (-) number.

Can you change the script to make the blue sprite jump higher, or pause for longer at the top of the jump?

Step 3.5

If on edge, bounce

Open **CD Resource 3d – Edge bounce**. This script block makes a moving object **bounce** off the edges of the game screen.

Does the object always bounce back in the direction it came from? Can you predict how the object bounces?

Step 3.6

Screen coordinates

The **Stage** in Scratch is divided into an invisible Cartesian grid as shown on the right. Every point on the grid can be identified using **coordinates**. These are two numbers, one that defines the horizontal **(x)** position and one that defines the vertical **(y)** position. A coordinate is written **(x,y)**.

You can use coordinates to reset a sprite's position at the start of a game, jump or slide sprites to different positions during a game, and restrict movement to certain areas of the screen.

CD Resource 3d – Coordinates shows some of these functions in action.

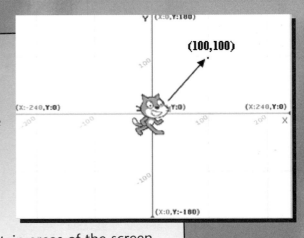

Step 3.7

Restrict movement to certain areas

Sometimes you may need to restrict the movement of a sprite to a certain area of the game screen. You can do this using the coordinates of the screen. The script in **CD Resource 3d – Restricted movement** allows movement of the sprite so long as the sprite's vertical position (y position) is greater than zero (0).

When the sprite attempts to move into the lower half of the screen it is prevented from doing so.

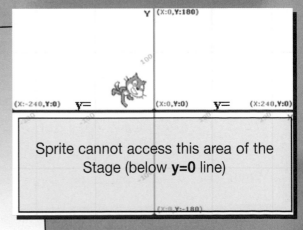

Sprite cannot access this area of the Stage (below **y=0** line)

GamePlan IT

Tutorial 4 Game play

This is probably the most important aspect of game design. You need to ask questions such as: What is the object of the game? How does the main character move within and interact with the environment? Are there points to collect, objects to find, destinations to reach or special powers to discover? How is the player kept informed of progress throughout the game?

By the end of this tutorial you will be able to:

- Consider different types of game play and user feedback
- Apply coding techniques to create interaction and feedback in Scratch games

Step 4.1

Sequences of events

Think about your favourite computer game. What exactly happens in the game and in what order?

A programmer has to have a very clear idea about what each element of a game does. Things will also happen in a set order, or **sequence**. A simple sequence is shown on the right.

Scratch allows you to build these sequences using script blocks. Open **CD Resource 4e – Banana Shoot** and play the game.

Player presses space bar
↓
Ball moves vertically up
↓
Ball hits fruit
↓
Fruit disappears and sprite thinks 'Yum, bananas!'

Step 4.2

'If' statements

In computer games there is often more than one possible outcome to an event.

Open **CD Resource 4c – FrootShoot!** In this more complex game, when the Bertie sprite shoots a missile there are two possible outcomes:

a. The missile hits fruit and the player gains points
b. The missile hits junk food and the player loses points

In this game, the **IF** statement enables two possible events to happen, with different consequences.

Sprite 1 shoots missile
↓
Missile moves vertically up
↓
IF
↓   ↓
Missile hits fruit   Missile hits junk food
↓   ↓
Fruit disappears   Food disappears
↓   ↓
'Yum' sound plays   'Belch' sound plays
↓   ↓
Score goes up 50   Score goes down 100

Step 4.3

Write a sequence for your game

Now write a similar set of instructions for one of the game play events in your own game.

When you build the game in Scratch, the instructions will be different, but follow a similar sequence.

Step 4.4

User feedback – 'think' and 'say' scripts

Scratch has script blocks to enable sprites to 'think' or 'say'.

This can be used for various purposes, for example, to show that a hit has been scored.

Look at the feedback thought bubble in the Banana Shoot game. Could you use this in your game?

Step 4.5

Broadcast scripts

The programmer of the Banana Shoot game has used a **broadcast** script to tell the character when to display the thought bubble – i.e. when the ball hits the bananas.

Broadcast scripts work in two steps. In this example:

Step 1: The banana sprite broadcasts the message 'banana hit' when it is hit by the ball sprite.

Step 2: The Bertie sprite receives the message that the banana sprite sent and thinks, 'Yum, bananas!'

Step 1

Step 2

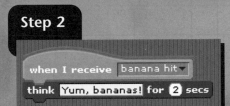

Step 4.6

Creating variables

The most important feedback to give a player is the current state of the game. This could be the current score, health or number of lives left.

Values, like score or health, that change throughout a game can be controlled by **variables**. These scripts can contain numbers or text that can be programmed to change when things happen.

Choose **Make a variable** and give it a name, for example, 'Health'. Set the variable to a value of your choice at the start of the game.

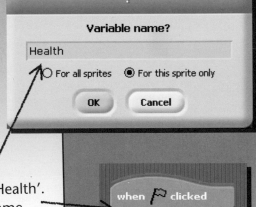

Step 4.7

Changing variables

You then need to program the variable to change when certain things happen. In the example, the player's health changes when Bertie 'shoots' the bananas (when the ball sprite touches the banana sprite).

Try creating a variable for your game.

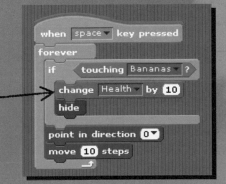

Tutorial 5 Maintaining player interest

Successful computer games all have common elements. For example, many are highly addictive so that you don't want to stop playing them! They start easy and get harder. As the game progresses, new levels, different environments, faster opponents and harder challenges are introduced. These elements are essential in order to maintain player interest throughout the game.

By the end of this tutorial you will be able to:

- Explore different ways of maintaining player interest in games
- Use Scratch to program simple game difficulty
- Create additional levels in Scratch games

Step 5.1

Set difficulty level in games

Open **CD Resource 5a – Difficulty levels**. This game allows the player to choose the difficulty level at the beginning of a game.

The **Easy** and **Hard** buttons are sprites containing scripts that control how fast the food falls.

Look at the scripts in this game. The programmer has made a variable called 'fallspeed'. Clicking on **Hard** sets the fallspeed variable to be twice as fast as clicking on **Easy**.

It is good practice to set the starting value of variables at the beginning of a game – this is called **initialising**.

Step 5.2

Changing variables during game play

Open **CD Resource 5a – Variables**. In this game the object is to eat all the food items as quickly as possible. Each food item affects the sprite's speed in a different way. Junk food items slow him down and fruit or vegetables speed him up.

'Speed' is programmed as a variable, so it changes when Pacman reaches each food item.

There are also 'Timer' and 'Health' variables in this game. Can you see what each of these variables is programmed to do?

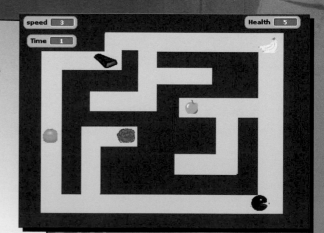

Tip: Try to keep it simple. You can have too many variables in a game, and for younger players this might make it too complicated.

Tutorial 5 Maintaining player interest

Step 5.3

Challenging times

Many computer games are played 'against the clock', for example, in racing games. The player is challenged to try and beat their best time or the best time of other players.

A similar idea is where the player must complete a task while the clock counts down. How could you amend the 'Timer' script in the Pacman game to count down the time from 60 to 0 (zero) seconds?

Step 5.4

Keeping the score

Players usually like to keep track of how they or other players are doing in the game. One way of doing this in Scratch is to use the **Make a list** script blocks (on the **Variables** menu). With 'lists' you can add 'values' such as numbers or text to any position in the list.

In this example, the last five scores can be recorded on screen.

The script (right) could be adapted to show the last five highest scores. Think about how you could do this.

Tip: The broadcast script block can be used here because it allows an endgame signal to be sent to the list.

Step 5.5

Add new levels

All game players love to complete a level in a game. They look forward to new challenges in subsequent levels, for example:
- Different environments and backgrounds
- More special features or powers
- Higher degree of difficulty

Open CD Resource 5a – New level and compare it to **CD Resource 5a – Difficulty levels**. It is the same game, but with a new level added. What new challenges have been added?

What new challenges can you add to your game?

8.5 GamePlan IT

Tutorial 6 Game distribution

Creating an effective distribution chain for a computer game is absolutely crucial to its success. Even really well designed games can fail to reach the target audience if they are not distributed effectively. The timing of a game release can also be important, for example, to coincide with a film or a specific calendar date.

By the end of this tutorial you will be able to:

- Discuss the pros and cons of different distribution methods
- Decide on the most appropriate platforms for game development
- Agree on a licensing deal that makes sense for the new computer game

Traditional methods

Early computer games were mainly distributed via amusement arcades. Arcades have become less popular in recent years, although in some countries they still have a huge following, for example, Japan.

Retail outlets

Another traditional method of selling computer games is through chains of shops such as HMV or Zavvi. Some shops have a trial facility that allows a buyer to try a game before they buy it.

Online delivery

Nowadays, millions of computer games are sold over the internet. Prices are cheaper than in shops because there are fewer overheads, for example, rental of shop space. Games are also easy to download from the internet.

Companies often require a user to sign up with their email address in exchange for free games.

Step 6.4

Viral marketing

Sometimes companies use a technique called 'viral marketing' to sell their product. This relies on people telling their friends about products they like.

Traditionally this happens naturally via 'word-of-mouth' but nowadays companies use social networking websites such as Facebook and Bebo. Users can 'forward to a friend' product website links or video adverts that they like.

Step 6.5

The mobile market

The development of games for the mobile market is becoming increasingly popular, for example, phones and a range of multi-purpose handheld devices. Such games are often quite simple and require only a tiny memory to run.

Perhaps Scratch games would suit this kind of platform – what do you think?

Step 6.6

Other distribution methods

A game that is educational, free and tied into a specific 'brand' or a market like the food industry could be distributed in some interesting ways.

A game about healthy eating could be distributed along with appropriate magazines or even with food products such as on the back of 'healthy' cereals.

FROOT SHOOT!

4+

This game is seriously good for your health!

Step 6.7

Target markets

A **target market** is the group of people you want to buy your product. They could be a specific age-group, gender or profession, etc. Some products will have more than one target market.

The target market will affect the way a product is distributed. Sometimes a target market is not obvious at first. For example, some residential homes for older people have started to buy Nintendo Wii games consoles, to improve their residents' fitness. How could you distribute Wii consoles to make the most of the older market?

Step 6.8

Decide which distribution methods to use

In your group, look at the different distribution methods listed and decide what the advantages and disadvantages of each method are. Remember to think about who your target markets are.

Then draw a mindmap diagram like the one shown on the right to show the different ways in which you could distribute your computer game, taking into account the needs of each of your target markets.

Toy shops

Target market: CHILDREN

UNIT

Unit assessment
Game concept

Introduction

GamePlan IT were very impressed with your design proposal for the new '5-a-day' healthy eating game. They now want you to submit a design proposal for a new educational game aimed at teenagers. They have sent a detailed description of exactly what they require in order to allow them to decide on whether to hire you to create this new computer game.

Teenage computer game - Message

File Edit View Insert Format Tools Table Window Help

Type a question for help

100% Read B

Send | Options... ▼ | HTML

To...   Year8programmers@programmersrus.org.uk

Cc...

Subject: Teenage computer game

Dear Year 8 programmers,

We loved your designs for the '5-a-day' healthy eating computer game. Therefore, we would like to invite you to submit a proposal and design for a new action-style game aimed at teenagers. We will leave the final decision about the theme down to you!

As you know, the computer games market is highly competitive and we need to ensure that all our new games are of the highest standard. There has been a lot written in the media recently about the effect of computer games on teenagers and you will need to convince us that your proposed game is both educational and suitable for the target audience.

The design proposal

Submit your proposal on no more than two sides of A4 paper. Word count should not exceed 500 words and there should be no more than six images in total.

Please ensure that you explain and show:

- any research that helped to influence your game design
- why it would appeal to the target audience
- the main technical difficulties and how you overcame them by excellent game design and clever use of program scripts
- how you intend to distribute the game to the target audience

Good luck!

W Kid

Managing Director – GamePlan IT

Unit assessment: Game concept

Assessment tips:

- Open a word-processing document and save it as **Unit 8.5 – Unit assessment** in your folder **Unit 8.5 GamePlan IT**.
- Start with a brief description of how your game is supposed to function.
- Explain clearly how this game suits the target audience.
- You should include brief details of any research about computer games and how this research has informed your game design.
- Your game design document must have written and pictorial evidence, for example, annotated screenshots of different parts of the game, examples of scripts that you created, etc ...
- You can achieve higher levels if you explain how you overcame any significant problems.
- Finish by suggesting what distribution networks you intend to use.

Tip: Remember to include screenshots of everything you did and annotate them with full explanations.

Glossary of key words

Avatar	A visual representation of yourself that is used within a digital environment such as a computer game or communication session.	**Drop-down list box**	A 'field' that needs completing with information; it sometimes allows a user to select from a number of different choices.
Chart wizard	In a spreadsheet, this allows a user to create quickly a chart from a particular set of data.	**Game classification**	A rating system given to some computer games that specifies the suitability of the content for different ages of games players.
Collision detection	When two physical objects touch each other, for example, a character/avatar and an object.	**Initialising variables**	This is where a variable is given a starting value in a computer program, for example, the starting 'health' of a character/avatar in a game.
Data validation	A way of checking data that is input into a program such as a spreadsheet, for example, checking that the data is of the correct type and format.	**Program bug**	A problem with game play, usually as a result of an error in the program scripts/code.
Design brief	A specification given to a designer about how a game should look and function.	**Variable scope**	Variables tend to be described as local or global in their scope. It is a measure of whether the variable applies to one thing, like an individual character, or everything in the whole game.

Model answer Level 5

Research and design

To achieve a Level 5 you will need to:

✓ Show how your research has influenced the style of your game

✓ Explain how your game design suits the theme and target audience

✓ Demonstrate how you overcame any technical issues

This script tells the broccoli sprite to go to its starting position, show itself and then fall when it receives the 'showtime' broadcast signal.
It also tells the broccoli sprite to 'hide' if it touches Bertie, and it tells the score to go up by 10.

I researched on the internet and got my friends to answer a questionnaire. Most of them said they liked fast action games.

My game is quite fast and has a character who has to catch food. He must catch the fruit and avoid the junk food. The player scores 10 points for catching fruit and loses 20 points for catching junk food.

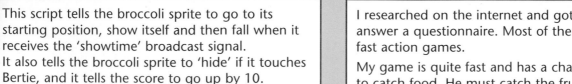

```
when I receive showme1 ▼
go to x: -39 y: 150
show
point in direction 180 ▼
repeat until    y position ▼ of Sprite2 ▼  < -100
    move fallspeed steps
    if       touching Bertie ▼ ?
        hide
        change score ▼ by 10
```

Teacher says:
This student has used effective scripts to control the basic game elements such as movement, collision detection, sprite appearance, keeping score, etc.

She has thought creatively about how to solve obvious problems such as what happens if fruit is not caught and falls to the ground?

```
when ⚑ clicked
forever if   key left arrow ▼ pressed?
    move 10 steps
    point in direction -90 ▼
```

```
when ⚑ clicked
forever if   key right arrow ▼ pressed?
    move 10 steps
    point in direction 90 ▼
```

Teacher says:
This game is suitably simple for the target audience (children) and children will be familiar with the keyboard controls.

There is a clear aim that supports the 5-a-day campaign by changing the 'score' appropriately, depending on the food item collected.

This script moves Bertie left and right with the corresponding arrow keys. Children are used to controlling movement with these keyboard controls.

Model answer Level 5

Evaluation and distribution

To achieve a Level 5 you will need to:

✓ Show that you have considered weaknesses in the game

✓ Explain how you would want to develop the game further

✓ State how you intend to distribute the game

My game was a bit boring because it was easy to know where the fruit was going to fall. I decided to make 'Easy' and 'Hard' versions so that the player could choose.

I did this by making two sprites, one for the easy game and one for the hard game. I also made a variable called 'fallspeed' which is the speed the food falls at. When you click on the 'Easy' sprite the fallspeed is slow and for the 'Hard' version it is faster.

Teacher says: *The game is a little predictable. The student has thought about this and considered how to add a bit of variation.*

Foods have different effects on the body and it would have been a good idea to make different foods carry a different value (rather than just + or − 10).

Allowing the player to choose a difficulty level is a good idea.

To make my game more interesting I think I would try to make the food fall more randomly so you don't know where it's going to fall from. I could also make some new levels that are harder.

I ought to include some more levels as well, but I didn't have time to do this. I also need to write a script that knows when the game is over.

Model answer Level 6

Research and design

To achieve a Level 6 you will need to:

✓ Give evidence that shows how your research has influenced the style of your game

✓ Explain how your game design is especially suited to the theme and target audience

✓ Demonstrate how you overcame or intended to overcome all the technical issues

✓ Show that you have considered different distribution methods for the game

Strategy	Action	Shooter	Sports	Arcade	Puzzle
2	6	8	2	4	1

I sent a questionnaire to a primary school to ask what games children prefer. Most students prefer shooter-type games. My game is modelled on Space Invaders as research on the internet showed that this was one of the most successful games ever.

The aim is to gain points by shooting healthy foods and avoiding junk food. I included a 'High Score' counter.

I included a catchy soundtrack and when the foods are hit, the player gets a 'yum!' or 'yuk!' sound.

Teacher says:
This student has done some effective research by using a questionnaire with the actual target audience.

This game is likely to engage young learners because it:
- *Is simple to play*
- *Has familiar game play*
- *Has a cool soundtrack*
- *Includes excellent user feedback*

score 150   HighScore 300

Yum! 50 points

Foods cross the screen at different speeds.

The player's character moves left and right with the arrow keys and shoots by pressing the space bar.

Teacher says:
Some of the scripting has been well thought through. The handling of the food types is very simple – only one sprite is required which changes costume each time it crosses the screen.

The student understands how to set the starting position of the foods and randomly assign different movement rates. This makes the game more interesting to play.

My game has six food types – three healthy and three not so healthy. The main food sprite has six costumes that can be chosen randomly.

This saved time as I did not have to put scripts into lots of sprites.

I can set the starting position of any food using its 'x and y' coordinates.

```
when ⚑ clicked
switch to costume strawberry
set foodNumber to 1
set startX to 250
set endX to -235
set startY to 50
broadcast food2Hide
```

Model answer Level 6

Evaluation and distribution

To achieve a Level 6 you will need to:

✔ Show that you have considered weaknesses in the game

✔ Explain how you would want to develop the game further

✔ State how you intend to distribute the game

I am pleased with the way my game is developing. There are still some problems with the scripts.

The game would definitely be better if there was a high score list. So, for example, the last 5 high scores could be shown along with the player's name. I think this could be done using the 'lists' script block.

Teacher says: *This game has a lot of potential.*

He has some interesting ideas for further development. Players like to know who got high scores and this motivates them to try and be the best.

It's a good idea to compress games as much as you can without affecting quality of graphics and sound too much. This helps internet distribution.

Getting the target audience sharing the game online is a great idea. Companies use this technique all the time, as they know popular games will be distributed for them.

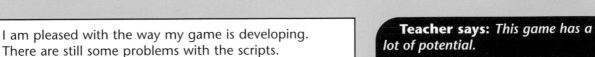

This script handles the shooting part of the game. The bullet sprite appears wherever the character is. I used the 'change y' script block to move the bullet upwards.

I saved different versions of the game, rather than just saving continually over and over on the same file. That way if I messed up I could always go back to an earlier working version.

This game has a graphic backdrop and a music track, so I compressed the game images and sound before final distribution. This keeps the file size down for internet distribution.

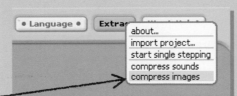

I intend to place a copy of this game on the Scratch website. I have also encouraged my younger brother to send it to some of his friends to play. He has a Bebo account and he could share it via this social networking site.

Mind your own Business!

UNIT

Unit introduction

In this unit you will work as part of a small advertising company, Way Out Productions, to devise a marketing strategy for a new healthy eating computer game aimed at children between 5 and 9 years of age.

Working as part of a team, you will need to allocate roles in order to meet deadlines. You will develop a project timeline and keep in regular contact with your client, GamePlan IT. The team will be expected to produce multimedia content for print, radio and TV.

Unit learning objectives

We are learning to:

- Fulfil specific roles within a larger team
- Use a spreadsheet to manage a project timeline
- Develop flyers and packaging for print
- Use videoconferencing as a communication tool
- Produce podcasts for radio and the internet
- Edit a promotional video for TV

Unit preparation

1. You will need to set up a folder in your area and name it **Unit 8.6 – Mind your own Business**.

2. You should be able to use simple tools in a spreadsheet.

3. You should know how to manage computer files and about different file types.

Start thinking about ...

Project management

Successful advertising agencies are generally composed of a team of highly dedicated and creative professionals who pull together in order to meet the tight deadlines set by their clients. Within all teams, however, individuals will tend to be responsible for a particular area of work. Take Way Out Productions, for example – their team is made up of:

- Project manager
- Publicity and communications officer
- Graphic artist/designer
- Digital media director/editor
- Media researcher

What do these jobs actually involve? Should one person only ever do just one job?

Step 1.1

Project manager

A **project manager** has overall responsibility for the success or failure of a project. She/he needs to have an overview of the progress of the project and check to see if the project is meeting deadlines.

Project managers need to meet with individuals in the team from time to time, encouraging and supporting them, even occasionally reallocating tasks where necessary. They need to have a flexible approach to any problems that may arise.

Step 1.2

Publicity and communications officer

A **publicity and communications officer** supervises all the print and digital communication elements for the team. This person may have to seek permission to use media elements (for example, video clips) in multimedia advertising campaigns.

He/she will also be the single point of contact between Way Out Productions and the client company – this may include letters, emails and videoconferencing.

Step 1.3

Graphic artist/designer

A **graphic artist/designer** designs page layouts and creates images for print and the internet. For example, flyers, logos, banners, packaging, CD covers, etc.

Step 1.4

Digital media director/editor

A **digital director** is responsible for planning and 'storyboarding' multimedia projects. The director needs to continually think about the target audience of a campaign. An editing role requires work with other team members to prepare audio and video content in preparation for final release.

Step 1.5

Media researcher

A **media researcher** needs to find out what other companies are doing, particularly in relation to the marketing of similar products. A researcher also needs to source relevant media for the company, for example, images, audio and video clips, etc.

Mind your own Business!

Tutorial 3 Packaging a product

In this tutorial you will focus on designing the packaging for your new computer game. The design of the CD box is important because it has to be eye-catching and appealing to the people buying the game.

By the end of this tutorial you will be able to:

- Create a 'net' or template for your box using **Microsoft Publisher**
- Create a design for your computer game packaging

Step 3.1

Nets for packaging

To create a box you need to create a **net**, an example of which is shown on the right. The net needs to include **tabs** that can be glued together when the box is folded into shape.

What shape box will the net on the right make?

Now draw a freehand sketch of a net for a box that would be a suitable size and shape for your computer game (the game will probably be on a CD or DVD).

Tabs

Step 3.2

Create a net in Publisher (1)

Open Microsoft Publisher and choose **Blank Publications > Full Page** as shown.

Then choose **File > Page Setup** and change the orientation to **Landscape**.

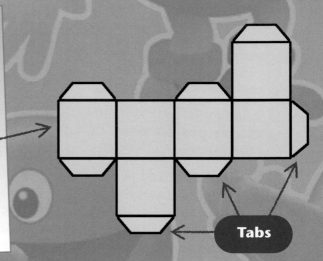

Step 3.3

Create a net in Publisher (2)

You will need to make sure that your net is the right size. Use the rulers at the top and left-hand side of the page to help you.

Following your sketched net, use the **Rectangle** tool in the **Objects** menu (left-hand side of the page) to draw the front of your box.

To make the back of the box, right-click on the shape you have drawn for the front, and choose **Copy > Paste**. Position the back of the box by left-clicking and holding on the shape. Then drag it into position.

Then complete your net, referring to your sketch.

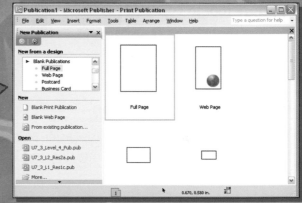

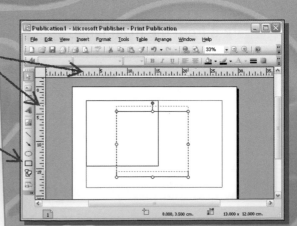

Step 3.4

Look at other designs

Having created the net for your box you can now start to design the graphics for your computer game packaging.

First, look at some examples of computer games boxes on a website such as Amazon (**www.amazon.co.uk**) and take screenshots. Paste your screenshots into a word-processing document and annotate them to show key features, such as title, characters and age range.

If you can get screenshots of the back covers too, include these for annotation.

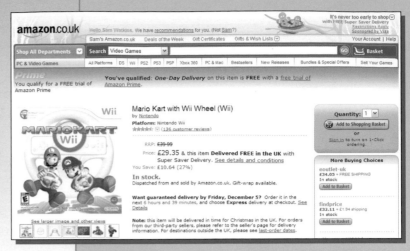

Step 3.5

Sketch some designs

Most designers do freehand sketches first to get a rough idea of what the layout of their design will look like.

Do two or three pencil sketches of different front cover designs. Remember to add in all the features you spotted on other CD covers.

Choose one design as your final design.

Step 3.6

Create a design in Publisher

Use your sketch to lay out your final design on your box net in Publisher. You can add shapes and text boxes to the page from the **Objects** menu.

To bring a shape in front of another shape, right-click on the shape you want in front, and choose **Order > Bring to Front**.

To colour shapes, use the **Fill Colour** tool. You can use **Fill Effects** to make a gradient fill, which will give objects a 3D effect.

Alternatively, you could scan hand-drawn images and import them into your publication.

Mind your own Business!

Tutorial 4 Holding a FlashMeeting

The world of business is increasingly reliant upon digital communication, and Way Out Productions is no exception! It can be very expensive to send people across the world, so more and more companies are using videoconferencing technology for holding meetings and giving presentations online.

By the end of this tutorial you will be able to:

- Deliver a presentation over a videoconferencing link
- Use a range of FlashMeeting tools

Step 4.1

Joining a meeting

When a meeting has been booked, a web address is created that you need to navigate to in your browser.

Then you will need to log in (using your registered email and password) or enter as a guest.

Note: Some features are not available if you only log in as a guest.

> **FlashMeeting**
> 3.2
> This meeting is being recorded
>
> Progressive Publishing 5-a-day publishing marketing meeting
>
> Enter your Sign In details
> E-mail   Remember ✓
> youremail@anywhere.com
> Password   Remember ✓
> ********
> Apply   for a new 'Sign In' account
>
> CONTINUE
> ● Enter meeting Signed In
> ○ Enter meeting as a guest
>
> Clear Port: 1935

Either sign in with your FlashMeeting details or 'Enter meeting as a guest'

Step 4.2

Allow camera and microphone access

You have to allow Adobe Flash Player access to your camera and microphone, so click **Allow**.

> **Adobe Flash Player Settings**
> Camera and Microphone Access
> flashmeeting.e2bn.net is requesting access to your camera and microphone. If you click Allow, you may be recorded.
>
> ○ Allow   ● Deny

Step 4.3

Last checks

You should now see this screen. If everything is working you should see your video stream in the small window and see the audio dial moving as you talk.

Set your **meeting name**, check the box **I agree to the terms** and click **ENTER**.

Note: You will not be able to enter the meeting until it is actually due to start!

Video and audio stream

Type your name here

> **FlashMeeting**
> 3.2
> This meeting is being recorded
>
> Progressive Publishing 5-a-day publishing marketing meeting
>
> Check Your Video & Audio
> High / OK / Low / Quiet
> Open Test Application
>
> Meeting open: time left 0:58:16
> Enter your name in the box below.
> yournamehere
> ENTER
> ✓ I agree to the terms
> You are Signed In to this meeting.

> 1.03
> **FlashMedia Test**
> Select the equipment you have conne...
> 🔊 I have speakers/headphones ☐
> 🎤 I have a microphone (either separate or with a webcam) ☐
> 📷 I have a camera ☐
> Now test my equipment

Click here to agree to terms

Tip: You can test your equipment by clicking **Open Test Application**

Step 5.4

Add different tracks to

You can record the three p... different tracks in Audacity...

Track 1: First, record your... speak clearly and put lots o... of voice! When you have fi... the track back to make sure...

Track 2: To add a pre-recor... **Project** > **Import Audio.** ... appear under the first track...

Track 3: To record another... button. A new track will be...

Step 5.5

Moving tracks

Use the **Time Delay Too**... the Timeline as you wish,... music to come in earlier t...

You can also set the volu... **slider control** at the he... balance the overall sound...

Step 5.6

Creating a podcast

Once you are happy with t... you can create it as a **podc**...

Podcast is a buzzword to d... concept: an audio or video... internet for you to listen to... a podcast is relatively simpl... export files in the correct fo...

To create a podcast we nee... format. To export a record... choose **File** > **Export As M**...

Step 5.7

Publishing your

To publish the po... **FTP (File Transfe**... available from a v...

Step 4.4

How FlashMeeting works

In the FlashMeeting software, only one person can talk at a time. However, everyone will be able to see and hear this person talking.

When you want to talk, click the **broadcast** button and you will join the queue to talk. When it is your turn, the broadcast button will turn green and everyone will be able to hear your contribution.

You must remember to click the button again when you have finished talking so that the next person can have a go.

Step 4.5

Use text chat

While live videoconferencing is taking place, other participants can be **text chatting**. To do this, click the **chat** tab to open the chat window. Be aware that these conversations can be seen by everyone at the meeting.

Step 4.6

Other tools

There are other tools you can use in FlashMeeting. One of these is the **FlashBoard** tool. You can upload media such as pictures on to this board.

This is very useful because you can draw or write comments on to the board and everyone can see everyone else's contributions as they happen.

There is even a tool that allows you to vote on important issues.

Tip: One of the great features of FlashMeeting is that anyone can go back and watch the whole of the meeting again. You can even see all the text chatting that went on!

To see the FlashMeeting recording, just go back to the original 'meeting' web address (URL).

Participants at the meeting

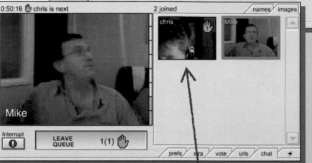

When you are waiting your turn, an orange hand appears informing everyone that you are next in the queue

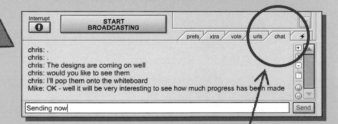

Click the chat tab

Participants can draw and write on the FlashBoard

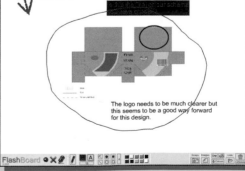

UNIT

Tutorial 5 Creat

Part of your marketing car
for the healthy eating com
computer game company'
networking sites.

In this tutorial you will foc
to record and edit sounds,

By the end of this tutoria

- Create a podcast and ac
- Experiment with effects
- Understand how to pub

Step 5.1

Getting started with

Click on the **Audacity i**
starting screen has a larg
controls at the top. Choo
Track to open a blank t
make a new recording.

Make sure your microph
this is working by record

Step 5.2

Quick reminder – the

Here is a close up of the
controls are very typical
(videos, DVD players, etc

The **Selection Tool** is als
you to select areas of the

Step 5.3

My podcast

Your advert needs to i

- A snappy message ab
  and where you can p
- Music to add atmosp
- Any other audio you
  or you could record s

One of the great advan
separate tracks, so you

SMART SKILLS BUILDER

2nd Edition

Revised for the renewed Framework and Key Stage 3 curriculum for ICT

A Student's Book, Teacher's Book and CD-ROM is available for each year group at Key Stage 3, providing:

- **Comprehensive coverage of the new Framework and National Curriculum**
- **Fun, student-friendly themes and activities to motivate students of all abilities**
- **Clear, colourful step-by-step walkthroughs of skills to be used as a reference book at the computer**
- **Creative and easy-to-follow teacher-written lesson plans**
- **Editable files and resources for students, including spreadsheets, word-processing documents, database files and image banks**
- **Model answers at different levels**
- **Unit assessment activities allowing students to develop their skills independently and teachers to assess progress**

The Smart Skills Builder for ICT series will progressively develop students' skills and capability across Key Stage 3, and help to build them into strong, confident and creative users of ICT.

For more information, or to order approval copies of any of the Smart Skills Builder for ICT resources:
Telephone Smart Learning on **01223 477550**
Email us on **admin@smart-learning.co.uk**
Or visit our website **www.smart-learning.co.uk** and place your order online